God Seen in the Mirror of the World

GOD SEEN IN THE MIRROR OF THE WORLD

An Introduction to the Philosophy of God

Pierre-Marie Emonet, O.P.

Translated by
Robert R. Barr

A Herder & Herder Book
The Crossroad Publishing Company

This printing: April 2016
The Crossroad Publishing Company
www.crossroadpublishing.com

Original edition: *Dieu contemplé dans le miroir des choses*
© 1997 by Éditions C.L.D., Chambray-lès-Tours, France

English translation © 2000 by The Crossroad Publishing Company

Printed in the United States of America

Library of Congress Card Number: 00-104967

ISBN 0-8245-1873-X

Contents

Part 2

Part 3

Part 4

Contents

O good, holy natural reason!
—Raïsa Maritain, *Journal,* 133

Introduction

*Unless one were to consider being in things,
one would be unable to pass to the First Cause
of all being.*

—Jacques Maritain

We shall begin this book antiphonally, as if we were praying the Divine Office. Two voices, in turn, will each celebrate the same fact. But this fact is a mystery. Fifteen centuries apart, a father of the church, St. Augustine, and a Catholic poet, Paul Claudel, call to one another as they celebrate, in things, the power to raise the intellect to the divine substance itself.

> I regarded all things beneath You, and I saw neither that they absolutely are, nor that they absolutely are not. They come from You, my God. (Augustine, *Confessions* 7.11)

Thus far St. Augustine. For his part, Paul Claudel addresses God:

> What would they do, my God, all of these poor things, which subsist not? Unless it would be to bear witness, by their nature, which is to be born and to cease, that You are, here and there?[1]

Augustine and Claudel are seized with exultation at the fact that, seeing the "ontological" poverty of things—their destitu-

1

tion with respect to their being—they understand their extraordinary message:

> If the world spoke less of You,
> I should feel less of this terrible ennui![2]

In their eyes—those of the theologian and the poet alike—
the poverty of the being of things demands the immediate
presence of the One to whom the act of being belongs
absolutely. The existence of God is first of all required by
things. There must be, with things that are born and die, the
active, creative presence of Being Subsistent in Itself. This is
the view by which we shall enter upon what Aristotle calls
"philosophical theology" (*Metaphysics,* E 1026a.18). The contemplation of being at the heart of things projects natural reason above this world to God. Thus, Aristotle called a part of
philosophy "theology " (ibid.).[3]

We must insist: one enters upon "philosophical theology"—
or "theological philosophy"—only if things are regarded from
a very precise angle: that of their *being.* Therefore the first step
to be taken by the intellect that seeks to rise to God by its natural capacities will be to grasp this object, "being," at the core
of all things. It will be essential never to lose sight of the fact
that, in this book, things are evaluated only and solely in terms
of the weight of their *being.*

What do we mean by "regarding things in terms of the
weight of their being"? Contemplating this rose, for example,
as being, and explaining its being? We mean: It does not suffice to explain this rose in terms of the fact that it is this rose.
The individual rose that has preceded it and has given it its
seed, can explain that perfectly well. From this viewpoint, it
has its place in a series of roses, one after the other. But we
wish to go further, and to explain the *being* of this rose. For
this, we are obliged to emerge from the series of roses that succeed one another in time. Why? Because we are looking for

the cause of the "essence" and the "existence" of this rose. To look for that is to look for the cause within it of these two acts by which it exercises its being.

Now, in order for a rose to exercise these two acts, essence and existence, simply by itself, each rose would have to pass by itself from potency to act as to its essence, and pass from nothingness to existence in order to be. Now, in either case, it would have to proceed from a lack, a privation. Such a lack or privation is merely being-in-potency, and, even more sheerly, nothingness. Thus, a lack and privation will certainly not be able to play the role of a cause! No, there must be Another-Being-in-Act, in which are found the essences and the existence of all things. For this reason, one cannot explain "the being of this rose as being" without mounting to Being-Subsistent-in-Itself. Now, from the precise angle of "being," the things presented to our regard must each and all admit their insufficiency, their poverty.

The being of things falls short. This act is not possessed by things in plenitude. Because of this lack, the One who, in the purity of act, exercises "being," must come to their aid. One could address them in the vein of Moses to Israel: "If God has attached himself to you, it is not because *your being* is strikingly strong or brilliant. On the contrary, it is because your being is weak and poor. God elects to be close precisely to this 'incidental' people!"

But if this is the way things are—if God is so "necessary" to the being of things—then why do we not see him? Why can we not ascend to God directly, but rather approach him at an angle? Aristotle has answered, and his answer is beautiful:

> The difficulty lies within ourselves. Our eyes are like those of the owl. As the eyes of the owl are blinded by the brightness of daylight, so the intelligence of our soul is blind to what in itself is most evident. Now, it is evident that God is there, present with each thing, but he is too bright for our intellect, which is

bound to a body. For us, it is not possible to stare at this sun.
(*Metaphysics* E 1026a.18–20)

And St. Augustine observes: "I saw all things below You"
(*Confessions* 7.11). God makes himself known, but not in himself—only in the mirror of things. This is the reason for our
manner of knowledge of God. It is because of the poverty of
their "being" that the existence of God, acting in their presence and in them, is demanded. This truth made St. Augustine and Paul Claudel burst forth in song. But their exultation
is spontaneous. It is the part of the philosopher to "found" this
truth.

Therefore we now turn to two thinkers—a pure philosopher,
Aristotle, and a theologian, St. Thomas Aquinas. Aristotle has
already shown the natural intelligence a number of routes for
ascending to God. St. Thomas takes them up and completes
this effort of reason. St. Thomas has "five ways," which have
become classic. Each ascends from things all the way to God.
Has it always been made sufficiently clear that, as he opens up
each of these five paths, St. Thomas begins by underscoring
one of the aspects of the ontological poverty of things? And
yet it is by reason of this quintuple poverty that the active presence of God with each thing is demanded. In these five ways
opened up by St. Thomas Aquinas—which some find dry and
ultimately ineffective when it comes to modern intelligence—
there is an evangelical sweetness. Jacques Maritain has said of
the being of the metaphysician that, "like the great poor," it is
"hidden in light."[4]

What we propose to do in these pages is first of all to con-
vince the reader that the existence of God is *necessary* to things.
Let us be frank: being, in each thing, is surrounded by nothingness. Things have nothing in themselves, in their own
essence, to draw them up from nothingness and thereupon to

sustain them above it. This is what we should like to bring out in the first part of our undertaking. It seems to us that the poverty of the being of things is not frequently enough emphasized. We have become convinced that one must begin by setting it in relief at the beginning of each of the five ways. Cardinal Charles Journet liked to say that the "being" of things is a "begged being." Anyone contemplating it can understand that, in each thing, existence is the deed of the Donor of being: God.

The *Summa Theologiae* of St. Thomas Aquinas, and indeed all of his works, then appear to us in a new light. A recent book is entitled *Saint Thomas d'Aquin, maître spirituel* [Saint Thomas Aquinas, spiritual master].[5] Now, St. Thomas is a "spiritual master" already on the theological plane, we dare say. Has he not emphasized that it is precisely their poverty that makes things God's "creatures"? It is because they are "God's creatures" that they require the proximity of self-subsistent being in themselves. St. Thomas will say: "Creation is the very dependence of 'created being' with respect to its concrete Principle."[6] And Père Torrell, by way of commentary: "Between God as Cause of the world, and the beginning of the world, there is absolutely nothing."

And a passage from *De Potentia* says: "It is by the goodness of God that things have their being and that they subsist in their nature."[7]

Who fails to see that a teaching like this sheds a first illumination on the world?

This poverty of "being" in things has its counterpart in the manner in which we know the Essence of God. In part 2 it is our own poverty that we underscore. Our own poverty appears in the manner in which we stammer something apropos of the divine Essence. Our potential, inasmuch as we are delivered to the power of natural reason alone, is to ascend to God by denying of God the perfections (concrete attributes) present

in things. And this negation can bear both on the perfections
in themselves and the manner of existence that these take on
in things.

The essences that we encounter here below are enveloped in
nothingness: yesterday they did not exist; or they present a
potential being, which is a quasi nonbeing. They are to become
—to pass from potency to act. In this, they are not capable of
being the vehicle by which we mount to a knowledge of the
divine Essence. However, it is actually from things alone that
natural reason draws its thrust. Things surely do not permit us
to say of God what God is; still, they give us to say what God
is not in himself. We may quote this text of St. Thomas Aquinas:

> The divine substance, in virtue of its immensity, surpasses all
> forms that our intellect can attain, and thus we cannot grasp it
> by knowing "what it is" (*quid est*). Nevertheless we shall have
> some knowledge by knowing "what it is not" (*quid non est*). And
> we shall approach the more nearly to this knowledge as we
> shall be able, by our intelligence, to remove more things from
> God.[8]

Who does not see that this reflection contains an avowal of
the poverty of the means that we can employ in order to know
God? God does not fit into the pigeonholes of our concepts.

This poverty in the sphere of our knowledge of God is par-
alleled in the area of our power to name God. In our third
part, we attempt to raise to God the names that we can give
him. But here once more, the words at our disposal are very
poor and cannot hold the mystery where God is hidden in
inaccessible light. Among them, however, there are some that
can pass through all of the degrees of being without being
stopped by any of them. It is in the Absolute himself that they
find their actual roots:

> It will be the exclusive privilege of pure or absolute perfec-
> tions, that is, of those attributes whose notion does not neces-

sarily include some imperfection, to be able—but in traversing
a kind of death—to pass beyond the "as if," and the curtain of
external behaviors, in order to signify directly what God is as
such and veritably, what God is himself.[9]

Other words will be unable to pass this frontier that separates us from God. We do set them en route toward God. But
we subject them to certain accommodations. If these words
cannot as such be the vehicle of bringing the mystery of God
all the way to us, they can enable us to catch a glimpse of correspondences between the divine Acting and that of creatures.
A like manner of speaking safeguards the mystery by keeping
us in mind of the fact that God is the Utterly Other. How can
words so permeated with earth mount to heaven? Better than
the great words, they nevertheless say what God is not and
cannot be. And that in itself is a kind of knowledge.

Finally, in part 4, we say "how things are" in God. This part
will complete our view of the poverty of things. The whole
"being" of a thing has, first, its place of origin in the thought
and the willing of God. God is the artisan of things, the architect. We are fond of the text of Jacques Maritain that tells us
that things begin as ideas of God. Maritain observes:

> In God, ideas are not like our concepts—representative signs
> drawn from things, composed in order to introduce into a cre-
> ated mind the immensity of what has been made and of what
> is, and to conform this mind to existents independent of it. In
> God, ideas precede things: they create them. Therefore, in
> order to find some analogy of this, theologians compare them
> to the ideas of the artist.[10]

To expound this analogy is to say that the whole being of
things has its source in the divine thought, and that everything
depends first of all on God.

Then we may conclude. We shall do so by analyzing what
the relationships are of our world to God and of God to our

world. It is here that the philosophy of relation finds its first application. Of itself, relation posits nothing in being. Of itself, all of the perfection (the attributes of being) of a relative term is to relate it to another being. Of itself, by the relations it maintains with another being, these relations say nothing of its being in itself. Nor is the other being, the object of the relation, directly touched in itself by these relations. But it is certainly of relation that we must speak in order to express the mystery of creation. Since "the entire being" of a thing, its essence and its existence, has begun with a relation, its being depends, as we shall explain, on self-subsistent Being. God's thought and willing must conjoin for a new being to be drawn forth from nothing. It is God's creative activity, and only this, that justifies its being. But because God creates this being, nothing has "shifted," if we may so speak, in God, its First Cause. God cannot pass from potency to act. In God there is no "can be," no "can act." God *is* "being and activity" all at once. But on the side of things, on the side of the world, everything has changed. Everything happens from this side, since the world and each thing pass from nothingness to being. At every instant, a relation is born which is real from the side of the world, but which from the side of God is only a relation as we view things. It is our reason alone that binds this world to God. But in God nothing has changed. God knows not the slightest flutter: not the least ripple appears on the Ocean of Being.

We shall then say, as contemplatives, that the world appears to us "in the unheard-of splendor of its Edenic nakedness. A rose, all new and transparent, made of relations to God."[11]

Part 1

1

What Is the Act of Being at the Heart of All Things?

It is as if, plunging into the ocean, one found on its floor a magic mirror reflecting the sky.

—Jacques Maritain

ST. THOMAS AQUINAS teaches that natural reason embarks on the path that ends with God only if, in things, it pauses before their "being." To one desiring to follow him on this path, therefore, a very first question arises: What is this "being" of which St. Thomas is always speaking? This is the first point calling for clarification. What is "being"?

True, "being," as a noun, owes its origin to philosophy. Nevertheless, it is not the philosopher's private property. Everyone pronounces it, in its oblique forms. But we must say, very few make it an object of their research! Some, most often poets, approach its true content. Apropos of the appearance of the first butterfly of the season, or of the appearance of the first seedlings in his garden, poet Ramuz notes in his *Journal,* under the date of March 18, 1940:

> A first yellow butterfly, a first white butterfly—trembling here and there above the still gray soil of the garden. Still gray, all naked, but it has broken in one place, and I saw a tiny pink shoot, and again a very pale green one, try to push through this

11

crevice and succeed. . . . So frail but so courageous, weaker
than all else beside, and stronger.[1]

A spirit that surely did not want to be taken for that of a
philosopher! But what metaphysician has better described,
and with more delicacy, the act of being at the heart of things?
For what the philosopher calls the "act of being" is very precisely the act of the tiny shoot that fascinated Ramuz. Altogether obviously, its effort in pushing toward the light is
indissociable from its being. Now, such an act is reproduced
every day, every moment, in myriad individuals and according
to myriad species. We wondered what "being" is. We answer,
and this will be our first definition: "Being" is a primordial,
universal effort on the part of things to come to light.

This first of all acts in each thing, signified by the verb "to
be," the philosopher calls "essence." Jacques Maritain insists,
"Essence is fundamentally an act."[2] Why call it "essence"?
Because, in the impulse that seizes a thing at the moment of
its "thrusting" or "growing" toward the light, there is another
—but hidden—aspiration toward another act, even more fundamental. Indeed, a thing cannot labor with such ardor to *be
what it is* without aspiring with equal ardor to *exist*. It is for this
very precise reason that the philosopher calls the first act
"essence." The root of the term "essence" is *esse*, "to exist."
Now, in proportion as a thing of nature tends toward the realization of that which it must be—for example, to be a daisy—in
that proportion it tends to exist. The word "existence" signifies the act of a thing in maintaining itself above nothingness.
As we see, the very word "being" actually denotes two acts,
acts very different in themselves, but made in such a way that
they will fit together.

The answer we have given to the first question—What is
being?—necessarily leads us to a second, What is it to *exist*?

What is *existence?* The act of *existing* is also an object of metaphysics. Nor, we must admit, is its discovery reserved to the philosopher. Thus, in his *Journal,* under the date of June 28, 1921, Ramuz wrote: ". . . To make of the end of my life a canticle of farewell to the world and to existence."[3] To see existence is to see at work, at the heart of each thing, a force other than that of essence. It is to see the force that snatches things from nothingness and holds them above an abyss. Now, this force does not possess in itself the essence that nevertheless calls it forth as its complement. True, it has within it the strength to come *to be what it is,* a daisy. But it does not have the strength to come to *be.* And an immense sadness seizes the poet's soul: "It is not possible that everything have been made for naught."[4]

If we have turned to a poet in order to discover what there is in the act of being, we have done so for the sake of testifying that the vision of this act is not the private property of the metaphysician! To see this act is a gift that can be bestowed on all. Only it does not suffice merely to glance at it; this act asks to be contemplated. The mind must have the disposition that consents to let things themselves tell their mystery in its entirety. St. Thomas Aquinas has said that philosophy is "nothing other than the description of things in the soul" (*De Veritate* q. 11, a. 1). Now both of Ramuz's visions, of the essence of the little pink shoot and of its quasi-miraculous "existence," have the virtue of best extracting the fact that, in being, two forces intimately join. These two acts, essence and existence, call to one another in order to join in the remotest depths of things. That is the act of being!

It belongs to "philosophical" theology (Aristotle's expression, once more, *Metaphysics* E 1026) to go still more deeply into our question of being. The act of being, begun over and over numberless times, must be supported. Despite what we have said of its primordial force, it calls to "another act," another energy, a "pure act of *being*," as its vehicle. To establish this is incumbent on philosophical theology. We then learn that, in the natural order of things itself, God is always very close to things. They would not subsist without the divine attention. It is the active presence of God in them; it is the divine action in them, continuous and hushed, that gives things to be and to become what they are. This first part of our book proposes to demonstrate this.

2

The First Poverty in the Being of the Things of Nature

Nothing would be produced here below . . . unless everything in the created universe were to be open to the action of pure Act (which touches it, Aristotle said, without being touched by it).

— Jacques Maritain

I T IS ST. THOMAS AQUINAS, then, whom we ask to lead us along the ways on which the intellect can reach God. Aristotle writes: "The first and most evident of the ways is the one that concerns the movement of a thing" (*Physics* 8.6.258b.10, 259a, passim). The context clearly shows that he wishes to speak of the movement of generation of a living being.

It is from Aristotle that St. Thomas receives his view: the birth of a simple flower conceals a mystery. This mystery resides in the inner labor deployed by a flower in order to become a daisy, our first example. This is the labor of the essence by which it tends to become *what it is*. Its energy engenders a continuous movement. From seed to blossom, its growth is accomplished without interruption of the continuity: roots, stems, leaves, flowers, succeed one another in a profound unity. Now, such a movement is progressive. It never ceases to pass from the less to the more. There is more in the roots than in the seed, more in the stem than in the roots, more in the

15

blossom than in the stem. It is a passage from the less of being
to the more of being.

This fact, repeated numberless times, has been transferred
by Aristotle to the area of philosophy, as he expresses it precisely in terms of being. In the movement of generation of a
living being, Aristotle says, there is a continuous passage from
being-in-potency to being-in-act. For the philosopher, an acorn,
for example, is an oak-in-potency, an egg is a robin-in-potency.

When we begin to think in these terms, we discern that the
generation of a plant or an animal introduces us into mystery.
The being-in-potency, after all, could not be the reason for the
motion we discern. When we ask how being-in-potency is
defined, Aristotle replies: "It is neither of being, nor of non-
being. It is a reality *very close to being*" (*Physics* 1.7–8.191b.16–
17). St. Augustine, for his part, having also perceived the mystery of this reality, sees himself obliged to say: "It is something
that is and that is not, at the same time" (*Confessions* 12.6). At
all events, these attempts at a definition place in evidence, in
this reality, a poverty of being. And as far as one descends into
a can-be, one fails to find this force of which the thing has
need in order to pass to a more-of-being. One must necessarily appeal to *another* being, one in act, to intervene and communicate *its* act.

True, the senses fail to perceive this "other being." The
intellect alone discovers the existence of a *universal "Agent"*
(the "subject of an act") of all of the acts of generation in
nature. If this faculty has the name of intellect, this is to signify its power of "reading at the interior" of the sensible
datum (*intus* = "within"; *lectus* = a "reading"). It is within the
thing, but hidden in the sensible aspects of the movement of
generation, that this Pure Act operates.

This Act of being is a pure "intelligible." It is unavailable to the acts of the senses. Thus we see that the fact of the movements of generation by which the world is constituted and ceaselessly renewed is explainable only by the pure and universal energy of an Agent at work in the most secret depths of each thing.

In his *Physics,* Aristotle calls attention to the solicitous presence of this mysterious Agent: "There is a Being that, distinct from every thing, nevertheless envelops each, maintaining it with its action and its energy. For this Being, in every living being of nature, is the cause of the continuity of its alteration, that is to say, of its generation" (8.6.258b.10).

Aristotle says that this Agent "envelops" the movement of the growth of things. Now, the Greek verb used—*periechein*—offers other nuances as well: "to hug," "to enclose," "to protect." How can we avoid the sensation that, when Aristotle was writing that, he was seeking to evoke the tenderness of the Pure Act of being who would later receive his divine name, God?

3

The Second Poverty in the Being of the Things of Nature

*In touching with his motion the huge, swarming
population of beings, God thrusts them forward.*
　　　　　　　　　—Cardinal Charles Journet

HAVING CONSIDERED the irrepressible thrust of the things
of nature to their own limits at the time of the formation
of their being, of their construction of their essence, St.
Thomas Aquinas contemplates them at the moment at which
they surpass themselves in their specific action. With their
specific action, we remain in the domain of essences, since
action is their shadow cast upon the things that surround
these essences.

The domain of acting places the philosopher before a mystery. It reveals that, at the interior of being, a tendency resides
to "overflow," to communicate its "perfections" or concrete
attributes to other things outside itself. Thus, Rainer Maria
Rilke addresses a rose:

> Rose, thou, O thing of excellence, complete,
> who infinitely contain thyself
> and infinitely spread abroad, O head
> of a body absent by reason of surfeit of sweetness![5]

Indeed, the mystery of being and that of its acting find their
eloquent symbol in the rose. The rose is "accomplished" when

it folds back over its heart, petal against petal. And the more it "contains itself," the more its color and scent radiate. For an intelligence sensible to the mystery of being, action is revelatory of something like a "creative" power. This power, as well, has been sensed and expressed by poets. In the following lines, let us take special cognizance of the presence of the word "create." Rilke says more of the rose:

> Alone, O flower abundant,
> Thou *createst* thy own space.[6]

.   And Saint-John Perse for the bird:

> Creator of its flight, the bird
> climbs invisible slopes. It reaches the summit
> of invisible levels. And there it holds fast.[7]

What a burst of colors emerging from a stem supposed to be merely green or grey! Cardinal Charles Journet liked to say that if a stem could see its own beauty it would be utterly amazed. The blackbird sings suddenly and suddenly stops—a ray of truth flashing forth in a spirit that was arid a second before. Such are the marvels of "acting." The element of novelty comported in the action of beings is sometimes so intensely felt that the philosopher does not believe that this novelty comes from the power of simple things.

Malebranche, for example, a seventeenth-century philosopher, transferred all causality from things to God. "There is but *one true* cause because there is but one true God.   The nature and force of each thing are but the will of God."[8] Malebranche was unable to see that God secures in natural bodies the dignity of cause. He ought to have seen the labor of the very rose bush as it toils to produce roses at the end of its branches. And yet, to the observer of all of the immanent operations it produces, that labor is clear. But what Malebranche did understand is that the rosebush is *too poor* in its being to be the *sole cause* of the appearance of the roses and of their radiating action. Its poverty, indeed, is what calls for the succor of the causality of the First Cause.

It seems to us that we shall approach the truth if we here sum up the doctrine of the preceding chapter.

When a substance has accomplished the being that it is, it overflows and tends to communicate this act. The rose tends to communicate its scent, the bird to communicate its song. But, when it makes this gift, the being in question performs a passage from potency to act. No substance of this world is identical to its operation. But each substance does have "potencies of acting." The plant grows its roots, which will have the power to absorb nourishment from the soil. In the egg, the bird forms wings, which will support its flight. As we see, a substance of nature does not produce its action *immediately*. It begins by possessing "potencies" of acting. But, deep as we may sound a "power" of acting, never shall we find, in this being-in-potency, the energy necessary to render these "potencies" actual. Another Being, a Being-in-act, is necessary. But this other Being, this Pure Act, does not do the work of the rosebush in the manner that Malebranche thought. It arouses it by promoting it, *by enveloping it,* by assisting it in order to have it pass to act. As we see, it continues to be the poverty of the being-cause of the agents of nature that appeals to the causal activity in their case of the First and Universal Agent. That Cause activates them, but does not violate them. Rather, it accomplishes their most secret tendencies.

Along the lines he proposes for the journey of causality that will lead the intellect to God, St. Thomas observes that no action arises in nature without there being a whole constellation of efficient causes at work, "causes" in the ordinary sense of the word (*Summa Theologiae* I, q. 2, a. 3). A tree, for example, could not bear its fruit unless there were, contributing to this activity, light, heat, water, and nutritive substances in the earth. These cosmic, universal agents are required. Still, in the last analysis, it is not because of them that the bird sings and the rosebush forms its sweet-smelling blossom. The cause of the bouquet and the cause of the singing reside in the respective species in which these beings subsist. Cocteau used to say, "Every bird sings in its genealogical tree." A contemplative has expressed this point, that of God's action on things, with rare insight and sensitivity. "When God summons forth a new reality, first he does not act 'on' things, or 'against' them (as we are obliged to do), but 'in' them, and He arranges it that 'everything' conspire, and this from the first moment of the universe, to produce the nascent being."[9]

Indeed, the causality of the substance of the blossom, and that of the bird, the causality of all natural agents, will not pass to the act of producing the scent and of making the song well forth, unless the First and Universal Agent makes each and all accomplish such a passage for their own part. We must come right out and say it: "Nothing would be produced here below unless nature were open to the action of Pure Act. Pure Act, Aristotle said, touches the world, but without being touched by it."[10] In touching by his motion the immense, teeming population of beings, God thrusts them forward. He was already "thrusting them forward" in their act of becoming such and such an essence: a rose, a swallow. He "thrusts them forward" again by constituting the vehicle of the communication of their riches to other beings by the radiation of a specific activity.

As we see, then, it is indeed on account of a poverty in their activity—that is, because they must pass from potency to act in order to act—that things summon to their presence the elevating action of the First Cause—a title that we give God.

4

The Third Poverty in the Being of the Things of Nature

*What would they do, my God, all of these poor
things that do not subsist, other than, by their nature,
which is to be born and to cease, to testify that
you are everywhere?*

—Paul Claudel

"ALL OF THESE POOR THINGS"! As we see, the poverty of things has held the gaze of the poet. This poverty is discovered by that poet in the fact that they have begun to be and will cease to be. Now, let us observe that this is the same reason as that advanced by St. Thomas Aquinas when he opens the third way that the intellect can follow in order to ascend to God. St. Thomas writes: "Among things, we find those that can be and can not be; also those that are born and that die. They can exist; they can not exist" (*Summa Theologiae* I, q. 2, a. 3).

In the two chapters immediately preceding, the poverty of things of which we have spoken was that of their essence. They have to "come" to being. They have to build themselves by stages at the time of their generation, when they move toward flower and fruit. The plant accomplishes the latter by a continuous movement. But it is a passage from being-in-potency to being-in-act. One must read the *Physics,* book 3, where Aristotle attempts to say what being-in-potency is. He needs three verbs: it is, he says, "a reality adjoining being, a reality that tends to being, that desires being" (1.192a.5–20). If we observe closely, these three verbs actually connote a lack, a deficit, a need. In the substances of this world of becoming, being evinces a "poverty." And it is because of this "lack," manifested by every essence, that things in formation require the assistance of the Being in which there is not the shadow of a lack: Pure Act!

But what St. Thomas and Paul Claudel are saying no longer relates to essence. It now relates to existence. But in order to fill the gap of their poverty—and another reason besides the presence of God with things—it must be, to begin with, that "existence" ceases to be a prosaic, pointless datum: "The essential," Maritain says, "is to have seen that existence is not a simple empirical fact, but a primitive datum for the mind."[11] How does it happen that, most often, we are blind to the most important element in things?

As we have explained in our first chapter, being, which is the sole object of our research, is constituted by two primordial acts that support all others. What appears to us in the very first place is essence—that is to say, the act by which a thing becomes *what* it is! Essence is the act by which a seed is to become a daisy, a bird's egg is to become a titmouse. It is clearly in essence, then, that the intellect is first interested. "The intellect scents essence," writes Paul Claudel.[12] But what about the other part of being: what about existence? Existence is also an act that essence cannot give itself. Essence, which has within itself the power to make itself be *that which it is,* remains totally incapable of making itself *be.* A rose can give itself its roots, its stem, and its petals; but when it confronts existence it is impotent. Were existence in the program of its essence, it would not have delayed to appear. But it was born yesterday and will die tomorrow. Nor does essence have the strength to keep its existence. The poet then asks with anguish:

> O rose!
> What a marvel! When we breathe this scent
> that sustains the gods,
> do we arrive only at this small, insubsistent heart
> that, seized amidst the fingers,
> loses its leaves and withers?[13]

Things' poverty of being as to their existence has a name: *contingency.* Now, one endowed with a lively perception of the contingency of the things of our world experiences the need to search beyond this world for the source of the existence of these things. There must be, outside of them, another Being— that is, the Being who is subsistent-in-himself. Existence is that force that snatches things from nothingness. Since yesterday they were not at all and tomorrow they will be no longer, existence must make them emerge from nothingness. But when they come, they appear from a point of departure in an antecedent nothingness. There will be a nothingness afterwards. In the last analysis, it is necessary that Being-without-nothingness draw them from nothingness and hold them above nothingness. It sometimes occurs that, instead of coming to the mind by reasoning—our manner of attaining it here—this truth suddenly comes by way of the mode of intuition. Raïssa Maritain recounts how, while traveling on a train, she felt the presence of this "Other Being."

> I was looking through the window, thinking of nothing in particular. Suddenly a great change occurred in me, as if, from the perception of the senses, I had passed to a perception entirely interior. The trees flashing by had suddenly become larger. They had acquired an immense dimension in depth. The whole forest seemed to speak, and to speak of Another.[14]

Let us sum up. The first two arguments, based on the becoming of being as essence, has us say: All things in their genesis and in their specific action suppose the *enveloping* presence of God activating them and helping them attain their full measure. The argument of the third way is based on the contingency of being, on another poverty, on a total poverty. What imposes itself on the intelligence this time is the *penetrating* presence of the same God. But why say "penetrating" presence? Because of all perfections—concrete attributes—existence is that which is most intimate and deepest in things. And since God *alone* is the source of existence and gives it ceaselessly, it is in things' inmost recesses that he is present. God must be present to each thing. At no moment of their duration could things give themselves existence, this absolutely first perfection. At the very heart of all of the "beings" of this world, God communicates this act uninterruptedly—from their birth to their death—and preserves it. Let us listen to the prayer of the metaphysician:

> And You who are perfect Being, You have not
> prevented me from being as well!
> You see this person I happen to be, and this being
> that I take in You,
> O my God, my being sighs for yours! . . .
> I see plenty of ways of not being,
> but there is only one sole way of being,
> which is to be in You, which is Yourself![15]

I can take Being only in You!

5

The Fourth Poverty in the Being of the Things of Nature

*The intellect compares things because it is balanced
on a divine point, inner, intangible. . . . And on the
simplicity of this point upon which, as on an invisible
fulcrum, it balances the universes. . . .*

—Dom Vermeil

T HE FOURTH WAY that the intellect can take to ascend to
God presents a certain similarity to the first. In the first
way, as we have shown, the intellect considers the movement
of generation of a body: the movement of the seed ends with
the flower. In order to cover this distance, the seed passes
"from the lesser to the greater," "from less of being to more of
being." We have had to conclude to the contribution of a superior source, conclude to the existence of a Being in Pure Act
in which resides the raison d'être of such passages. We do not
see this first Agent. And yet its presence is necessary. Let us
have an analogy.

> Suppose there is a glass tube protruding from the wall, and
> suppose I see in this tube a quart of water. Then I see the water
> level mounting in the tube—two quarts, three quarts. I shall say,
> "Someone is pouring water behind the wall and raising the
> water level in this tube." And suppose you tell me, "You have

no right to say that, you do not see that person." And indeed I do not see that person with my eyes of flesh, but I see him or her with the eyes of my intellect: "More cannot come from less." Thus, there is a source that raises the level of being.[16]

As we see, there are great mysteries behind the sensible appearances of things!

In this fourth way, which we shall follow, we find these adjectives of comparison: "less," "more." But, in this way, they are used to signify other relationships, relationships that appear on a static plane. Here is how St. Thomas Aquinas begins the presentation of this way: "We observe, in things, more and less good, more and less true, more and less noble" (*Summa Theologiae* I, q. 2, a. 3, fourth way). No one will deny that such comparisons fill our daily conversations! As for philosophers, they recall these expressions in order to sound their depths. In these expressions, where other persons see but daily banalities, the philosopher perceives the affirmation of a virtually recognized perfect Being!

Plato was the first to notice that an Absolute was hidden, and at the same time revealed, in such formulas. It is apropos of expressions like "more beautiful, less beautiful" that he drew his philosophy of *participation*. First he was struck by the fact that the attribute of beauty was universally evoked in our propositions. We attribute it in the domain of bodies, but also of moral actions, and even in the domain of the sciences. The intellect discovers the ocean of beauty, then, and at the same time infinite degrees of realization with, precisely, more and less.

These numerous degrees in the perfection of beauty are offered to the intellect like rungs for climbing. This perfection, or concrete attribute, which is the prerogative of no category of being, resembles Chagall's angels rising and

descending with perfect ease on Jacob's ladder! The same
must be said of other perfections, in which a similar virtue
resides: truth, goodness, oneness. Like being and the beautiful, the true and the good are available to the most diverse
realizations: in bodies, in souls, in spirits. This being given,
nothing prevents them from having elsewhere than in this
world of multiplicity and change a full and absolute realization
in some transcendent being. But for a like intuition to become
a conclusion, one must feel strongly that, here below, the realizations of these perfections are *really* limited, fragmented.
Precisely on the subject of beauty, Plato remarked:

> Things are beautiful on one day, but not the day after; beauti-
> ful from one angle, but not beautiful from another; beautiful
> here, but ugly there. In the world of our experience, they offer
> but a part of beauty to be seen. Therefore one must say that
> this perfection is "participated." (*Symposium* 210a)[17]

Next, St. Thomas, sharing the same view as Plato on this
point, extends it, saying that "since they have been participated, they have been *caused,* which is equivalent to saying that
they are not found by themselves, and thus that they are
caused by Another" (*Summa Theologiae* I, q. 2, a. 3, fourth
way).

This perfection of beauty, like that of truth, goodness, and
oneness, St. Thomas calls "inseparables from being" (*Commentary on the First Book of the Sentences,* dist. 8, q. 1, a. 3). Like
"being," they are transcendentals. This means that they traverse all of the categories of being, diverging toward infinity.
Here below, consequently, they can be found only in fragmen-
tary and varied state. It is like a mirror, shattered into a thousand pieces, but reflecting the sky nonetheless. And it is
among these myriad realizations that the intellect grasps these
degrees of more and less: "more *true,* less *true,*" "more *beautiful,* less *beautiful.*"

But how can the intelligence introduce these comparisons? It must already possess a criterion enabling it to measure degrees of participation in things. It is by reference to a fixed, secret point; it is by reference to an absolute center, that such comparisons can exist. To speak of more and less on the subject of perfections that of themselves are not limited to any category, supposes the interior vision of a transcendent reality. The intellect must be, as it were, pre-inhabited by the certitude that there exists, outside the finite, outside the limits of this world, a transcendent Being in which these perfections are found in purity!

To metaphysicians it is given—and herein resides their greatness—to gather in the things of this very world the witness that being, oneness, truth, goodness, and beauty have not here their native country. They are as in exile. In order to dwell here, they have had to don the *livery of the poor: matter.* Still, they cannot completely conceal the nobility of their origin, their birth. They cannot conceal from us that they have fallen from heaven. The metaphysician collects them. He sees that they are in things only as a part of themselves, and thus that they are *caused*—but not by themselves. He sees that they descend from Another Being, in whom they have their plenary realization. And therefore, as with St. Augustine, metaphysics ends in a burst of praise:

> It is you, O Lord, who have created these beings, you who are beautiful, for they are beautiful, . . . you who are good, for they are good, you who are, for they are. But they are not beautiful, they are not good, they do not exist perfectly as you, their creator. Indeed, in comparison with you, they have neither beauty, nor goodness, nor existence. (*Confessions* 11.4)

Yes, they are poor, and very poor!

6

The Fifth Poverty in the Being of the Things of Nature

It is very God, on high, who summons earth and water, who furnishes them with an idea of what is demanded of them and of what he intends to obtain from them.

—Paul Claudel

IN A FIFTH WAY by which human reason can also reach God, St. Thomas regards a final poverty at the heart of things. He considers how the substances of nature move toward their end: the grain of wheat for the spike, the egg for the bird. One certainly sees that they order their toil toward well-determined ends.

It is no less evident that they have not in themselves any knowledge of the end toward which they nevertheless strive with all their might. St. Thomas observes:

> We see that beings deprived of intellect nevertheless act in view of an end. This is manifest in the fact that always, or most often, they act in the same way and manner to realize that which is best for them. It is clear that it is not by chance, but in virtue of an intention, that they arrive at their end. (*Summa Theologiae* I, q. 2, a. 3, fifth way)

We gather the same impression when we take the trouble to study their organs. These beings are without knowledge, and yet they construct for themselves organs manifestly ordained to future quite determinate actions: the eye for seeing, the wing for flying, the mouth for speaking. One cannot then escape the sensation that there is, in this, the mark of an Intelligence at work in the construction of their organs. Aristotle remarks in the *Physics:*

> Spiders, ants, and animals of this sort seem to work with intelligence, or something analogous. To go a bit further, we see that, even in plants, useful things are produced in view of their end—for example, leaves for the purpose of shading fruit. If, then, it is by a natural impulse, and in view of some end, that the swallow builds its nest and the spider its web, if plants produce their leaves in view of their fruits, and guide their roots not upwards, but downwards in view of nourishment, it is clear that this sort of causality exists in natural generations and beings. (2.8.199.20–30)

It is impossible to doubt the existence of a "final" causality, an "end" in view, in the productions of nature. But the question that we must now ask is: Why does such a "finalized" action call for the presence *in it* of an Intelligence at work? Here is the answer: One thing cannot be ordered to another but by an Intelligence. Let us observe first that a thing cannot be set in relationship with another that would not exist. But, in natural bodies, at the moment of their generation, one sees an organ constructed *before* that thing that is its purpose. The bird, in the egg, grows wings and a pair of eyes long before using them. All of the organs of a living being are preordained to one of the activities yet to come. But one thing cannot be ordered to another that did not exist at all. This would be a contradiction. We must emphatically assert: if the organs that nature creates in a living being are ordered to altogether determinate activities, then these activities must exist. If they do not exist in reality, then they must exist in a thought. Indeed, for one and the same form, two manners of existence are possible: either in reality or in a thought.

Aristotle liked to say, "Before existing in reality, the house exists in a thought—in that of the architect" (*Metaphysics* Z 7.1032b.13–14). The same is to be said of all of the things of nature. They cannot be explained without the active presence in them of a transcendent, universal Intelligence.

We must add: The intention-of-the-end with which natural beings act, obviously, does not proceed from these beings themselves. The rose does not decide on the program to follow in order to come to being. Now, it is precisely this privation of knowledge that is, once more, one of the "poverties" of natural substances. It is precisely because of this privation that appeal must be made to an Intelligence outside of their nature —furnishing them, as Claudel says, with the *idea* of their development.

Aristotle was so struck by this mysterious, "finalized," energy that he himself invented the word that expresses it best: "entelechy" (in Greek, *entelēcheia*). Taken literally, this term means "have its end in itself." But one can have the end of activity within oneself only if one is its cause. This is the case when a person freely and personally determines the ends of her activity. But an end to be realized can be assigned to a thing by an Intelligence that thinks and wills it. This is the case with the things of nature. Because in themselves they were without intelligence, they can be ordered to an end only by an Intelligence transcendent to each and all, but operating in them.

It is indeed by reason of this *poverty* in the things of nature that there is demanded the presence of a universal ordering

Intelligence always at work. St. Thomas concludes: "There is an intelligent Being, then, by which *all* natural things are directed to their end, and this being is called God" (*Summa Theologiae* I, q. 14, a. 8). And he added: "God's knowledge is the cause of things. It is to created things as the knowledge of the artisans is to their works" (ibid.)

It is an Intelligence directing all things toward their end with power and sweetness—*fortiter et suaviter!*

Conclusion

*I was afraid that God would drop the universe
and it would smash to bits.*

— G. K. Chesterton

HUMAN REASON, by its very nature, has the power of actually reaching God, and first, this truth: *God exists.* In order to do this, St. Thomas Aquinas has traced out five ways. It is moving to see, in the Angelic Doctor, that it is of frailty, of poverty of being in things, that he asks they become the route toward this very first truth about God.

As we have seen, St. Thomas begins by considering the poverty in the essence of things—the act by which each thing toils in order to build what it is. Most often, it is after a lengthy effort that things come into being. Thus, the poet celebrates a rose:

> It is you who prepare in yourself
> more than yourself, your ultimate essence.[18]

To come to being, for this rose, requires time. By a continuous change, it must pass from seed to blossom. To avail ourselves of philosophical terminology in order to express this process, we shall say that it must pass from potency to act. But what is "being-in-potency"? With St. Augustine, we answer that

34

being-in-potency is a "quasi non-being" (*Confessions* 12.6). Now, it is from a starting point in this ontological poverty that the blossom commences its journey. And when it will have finished making itself be, when its essence is achieved, it must pass a second time from potency to act in order to exercise its action: to light up and perfume its space!

After the poverty of essence of a thing of nature, meta-physicians confront especially the poverty of existence. They see that the essences of things maintain themselves, but over an abyss of nothingness. This rose, yesterday, was not at all; and tomorrow it will not be at all. And we confront an even more basic poverty. G. K. Chesterton perfectly translates the sentiment that seizes the intelligence: "Everything could have not been." Everything that, in order to exist, has had to emerge from nothingness, "has escaped catastrophe by a hair."[19]

When we contemplate, in the light of metaphysical intelli-gence, these two absolutely first acts in things, essence and existence, the world surely seems "frail and fragile"! It cannot all by itself explain the being it exercises: "It has enough den-sity to pose the problem of its existence—but not enough to solve this problem by itself. For the being of contingent things is 'begged.'"[20] This is what can be drawn from a reading of this great article from the *Summa Theologiae* (I, q. 2, a. 3).

This emphasis on the radical poverty of being in things must not be interpreted as a disdain. Far from it. Like the poet, the metaphysician too is spellbound by what things offer to our contemplation. "The human being is born for contem-plation," says Ramuz.[21] By this he means the contemplation of things. Metaphysicians are the contemplatives of being in things. Still, they would be closing their eyes if they failed to underscore things' ontological insufficiency, that is, their contingency. It is because the world admits its ontological poverty that the intelligence sees itself obliged to take its leave of this world if it would seek its actual explanation. It finds it elsewhere. God approaches the poet and confides:

> Even before you knew it, I was there,
> And I remain with this person that I have made.
> You would cease to exist if I withdrew.[22]

Now, what God tells the poet, he can say to each thing! Each contingent being has need of the necessary Being. But let us be even more precise. In the line of existence, each thing owes everything to God. To come from nothing is to come empty-handed! In the line of essence, matters are different. Each thing is busied with being what it is: a rose toils to be a rose; it does not toil to be a tulip. But it is because God gives it existence gratuitously that it can work for its essence.

One must take the time to observe a flower, to regard the intelligent energy of which it makes use, in order to be able to assess how good it must be for it to be a rose, or a tulip. What gladness, if we may so speak, seizes the seed that, in order to come to light, bursts through the heavy cape of earth. How, then, could we fail to "see" that, if the Creator withdraws things from nothingness, it is in order that they may be able to give themselves their essence? Aristotle saw this. He said that Pure Act "envelops" things, in their becoming, in their genesis. And St. Thomas added that Act penetrates them and directs them toward their proper end. It is not in order to absorb them into God, as Jean-Paul Sartre thought, that God causes in them, immediately, their existence, but in order that they may be able to realize their tendencies—as the bird, to sing—and thereby to accomplish themselves fully. One day I asked a monk how his vocation had come to him. And he said to me, "My flowers were so beautiful, I had to go thank some-body!"

In this question of the existence of God, St. Thomas asks Aristotle for the contribution of his philosophy. Philosophers entertain certain purely metaphysical analyses capable of con-ditioning the natural intelligence to receive truths coming from above reason. They are truths that reason can also find, but they have come to it first of all enveloped in the divine light of biblical revelation.

Part 2

Transition

I T IS ON ACCOUNT OF the poverty of things that the intellect can find the reason for their being only by leaving this
world. Things are poor in their act of being. They are poor in
their very roots. Each of them, with the poet, could say to God:
"You see . . . this being that I take in you."[1] From whom else
could they receive it? In part 1, things have admitted this
poverty, that of their act of being, five times. Five times as well,
the intellect has produced a new golden thread bonding them
to God as to their First Cause. Let us understand well: It is
they themselves, things, that require God!

The Being that, at the termination of these five ways, has
appeared, has been given five names. These names, then, say
something of that Being, but always with respect to the world
for which it accounts. It has been called *Pure Act,* that is, Being
to which nothing is lacking. It has also been called *First Cause,*
that is, the cause on which all depends. It also has the name
Self-subsistent Being, that is, Being to which existence belongs as
its own property. *Absolute Being* is its name in light of the fact
that all things participate in it. Finally, it has been called *First
Intellect,* that is, Being that orders each and every thing and
leads it to its end.

It is surely clear that such attributes speak of a Being that cannot be found in the world, since none of the things that constitute this world responds to such definitions. Nevertheless, we must add at once that only such a Being is able to be found close to everything, in order to explain it, enveloping it in its Power, steeping it in its Presence, directing it by its Intelligence. Thus, it must be at once transcendent and immanent to the world. But can one enter further into the Realm in which these attributes are hidden? Can we know its Essence?

Before embarking on part 2, let us pause to see how St. Thomas sets us on the road to a knowledge of the Essence of God. We shall continue to follow him almost step by step, reading and commenting on articles 3 to 11 of question 1 of the Prima Pars of the *Summa Theologiae*.

With St. Augustine, he could say to God: "I had become altogether certain that your invisible beauties have been revealing themselves to the intelligence, since the creation of the world, through your works, and with them your power and your divinity" (*Confessions* 7.17).

To know the Essence of God—here is St. Thomas's aspiration, after having become certain of God's existence. His method will be the same: he will enlist the assistance of creatures themselves. To this end, he institutes a broad comparison between the way in which things come to the perfection of their essences and, on this basis, arrive at their radiation upon the beings that surround them—and then between the manner in which God, for his part, possesses his own essence and, in his turn, the manner in which he acts on the world of things. But after having given God, in part 1, attributes that remove him so far from creatures, how can we pretend to utter his essence?

7

How Utter the Essence of God?

In the blink of an eye, my intellect arrived at Being Itself. But I could not focus. My weakness recoiled.
— St. Augustine

HAVING DEMONSTRATED that God exists, how will the intellect not aspire to know more of him? This desire has come to dramatic expression in St. Augustine's *Confessions:*

> "What is God?" I questioned the sea and its abysses, and the living beings that move there, and they answered me: "We are not your God. Search above us." I questioned the blustering winds, and Air with his inhabitants, and he said, "Anaximenes is in error: I am surely not God." (10.6)

We have seen that the attributes that natural intelligence gives to Being, when it arrives at the termination of the five ways, declare how far God is above the capacities of this intellect. Still, we should like to know! Now, in the prologue to question 3 of the first part of the *Summa,* St. Thomas has specified what we can aspire to in this domain: "As we can know what God is not, and not what God is, we have not to consider how he is, but rather how he is not."

But we must be careful! St. Thomas is not professing agnosticism. He is not saying that we can know nothing of what God is. What he seeks to inculcate in us is what is called a *docta igno-rantia*, a "learnèd ignorance," a knowledge that knows that it does not know. It knows that the perfections of being that it contemplates in the realities of the world are found in God as in their First Cause. But it also knows that, in God, these perfections are not limited, fragmented, contingent, as they are here below! Natural reason does not have in itself the means of knowing such a Being. It avows its poverty, deciding none-theless to approach God while removing from him the limited, fragmented, contingent mode of these perfections. This will assure that natural reason will not commit the error of con-fusing God and the world! With Paul Claudel, it can say, "In the fact that I know him not, I recognize and know him." This is the proper manner of the intelligence in acknowledging and knowing the transcendence of God. It knows that it can approach the Essence of God, yes, but it also knows that it must do so by way of the *via negativa*, the way of negation. Because it is on an equal footing with natural things and their perfections, their attributes, natural reason admits that it loses its footing before God and the infinite divine perfections. It consents to being overwhelmed. It accepts being awash in the Ocean of the Divine Substance!

Let us say it once more: It is by the ministry of things that the metaphysician rises to God. To know God, one must begin by regarding the things God has made, and what God has given them of perfection in the roots of their very being. But natural intelligence cannot focus the Being of God Itself: "My weakness recoiled," St. Augustine confides to us (*Confessions* 7.18). St. Thomas Aquinas guides us to the divine Essence, but while teaching us to follow the *via negativa*. Before entering upon the quest, the intellect must efface from its mirror any-thing that could deform the image of God. First it undertakes a task of self-purification. But in doing so, it must never forget something else that the Angelic Doctor tells us: "As for the attributes whose imperfections we deny, . . . we refuse to ascribe them to God not as if God lacked them, but because God is too far above them" (*Summa Theologiae* I, q. 12, a. 12).

This observation preserves us from foundering in agnosticism. We must guard it for all of its precious worth.

8

The Perfect Simplicity of God's Being

> *. . . The rose, that under mortal winter and uncertain springtime composes, amidst its thorny leaves, the perfect, finally, red flower, in its glowing geometry.*
> —Paul Claudel

T HE ONE WHO SEEKS to know "who God is" is taught by St. Thomas, as we have seen in the preceding chapter, to remove from God what does not belong to God. But how are we to know what does not belong to God? We can say from the outset: they will be attributes contrary to those to which we have concluded at the term of each of the five "ways" that lead to the divine existence. These attributes are Pure Act, First Cause, and so forth.

With St. Thomas we plunge to the root of things, to their act of being, and learn how to compare things with the Act of Being that is in God, and how to remove from God all that does not belong to him. We shall follow him in the questions in which he establishes a broad comparison.[2]

And first, here below things *come* to be. They fashion, they constitute, they arrange their being. Indeed, in the act of being of creatures, in its roots, we find three distinct concrete principles: essence, existence, and subsistence. Let us briefly recall the meaning of these three terms.

Essence. In a rose or a swallow that comes to be, we witness the effort of toil by which they thrust to the light and construct their bodies, following a well-defined program. This primordial act is called "essence," from the Latin *esse,* which means "to be." In calling this toil "essence," we are stressing that essence tends to the existence in whose depths alone it can realize this program.

Existence. Since things come to be and pass away, we must distinguish their essence from their existence. If this rose was born yesterday and will die tomorrow, it is because existence is not part of its program. It cannot give itself existence—otherwise it would not have waited so long to exist! Existence is the other act of being besides essence. By existence, the rose is extracted from nothingness.

Subsistence. Subsistence is the perfection that, like a gold ring, separates one essence from another because it is attributed to this or that individual. Two daisies, for example, have the same essence, and yet this essence is received in each one as its own, so that it is incommunicable to the other. Subsistence is that which bestows on this daisy in the meadow the fact of being a subject of existence for itself.

Now let us "have a look" at the situation. Every being that we see in the universe "composes"—puts together—in itself and for itself these three principles that make it to "be."

We do not deny these three perfections, these three concrete attributes, of God. On the contrary, in God they have a perfect mode of realization. But in God they are in a profound oneness. None is "really distinct" from the others. Only our manner of considering them bases our giving them three different names in God. In the things of nature, essence and existence are "composed" as two really distinct acts, but acts also really conjoined, composed. In God, there is no composition—only an absolute simplicity. God never began to exist. God will never cease from existence. And God does not share the divine Being with another being. God is unique. In God there is no becoming, no change, and no multiplicity.

Paul Claudel observes that, in order to arrive at its red blossom, the rose needs time. And through time, its "composition" is uncertain. God, on the other hand, contains the flower of the divine Being without birth and without demise. God is the Rose of immediacy and constancy!

9

God above All Things, More Exalted than the Sun

The only created thing that we cannot fix our gaze upon is also the only thing that sheds its light on everything for us—the noonday sun.

—G. K. Chesterton

LET US CONTINUE to ask St. Thomas to introduce us into his own philosophical contemplation of God. Those who would doubt that metaphysics is a contemplation ought to read what Aristotle says of the study of natural being. In his treatise *On the Parts of Animals,* twice, only ten lines apart, he uses the word *theōrein,* which means to "see" a spectacle or theater piece. And he says that those who devote themselves to the study of different types of being experience marvelous joys, at least if they are capable of ascending back to the causes. For that is what it is to be a dyed-in-the-wool philosopher (*On the Parts of Animals* 645a.10–15). But one arrives at the philosophical contemplation of the divine Essence by following the path of negation—that is, in denying of God the imperfections one finds in the things of nature.

Having spoken of God's absolute simplicity—that is, of a divine essence that God need not "compose," an essence that has no "parts"—let us pause a moment to consider the action

49

of God. Let us set in relief the fundamental difference between the activity of God and that of things.

Let us take the example of a rose. When, after a lengthy labor, it achieves its essence, it contains itself perfectly. Then it illumines its space by its colors and fills it with its perfume. The poet questions a rose with great delicacy:

> Tell me, rose, whence it comes that,
> enclosed in yourself,
> your slow essence imposes
> upon this space, in prose,
> all of these airy transports![3]

Now we must observe: Here below, each thing acts within the confines of its species. The fig tree offers the sweetness of its fruit; the blackbird its melodious song. Cocteau says, felicitously: "The bird certainly sings in its genealogical tree." In comparison with this, what must we say of the activity of God? God, too, like all beings, performs a specific activity. But while the flower and the bird communicate an altogether particular, circumscribed good to other particular, circumscribed things, God has a universal, and therefore transcendent, activity. Why? Because the good that God communicates is existence, and all things participate in the existence bestowed.

St. Thomas writes: "As God is Being itself by essence, the proper effect of God is necessarily created being, as to burn is the proper effect of fire" (*Summa Theologiae* I, q. 8, a. 1).

Thus, God does not act as do creatures. Here we are in the *via negativa*. What God gives—existence—God alone has the power to give. And this is because God is self-subsistent Being.

Now St. Thomas adds, "Existence is the actuality of all things without exception, the actuality of all of the forms of being" (ibid., q. 4, a. 1, ad 3).

Besides the universality of the divine acting, we must conclude to the transcendence of that acting. The medievals compared God to the sun. As the sun ascends to its zenith and then spreads its influx of light and warmth upon all things, so God's influx is upon existence, in all of the forms of being, and in each one individually. God is the Sun of being. In Judeo-Christian religion, the divine activity is celebrated under that same symbol:

> Its rising is from the end of the heavens,
> and its circuit to the end of them;
> and nothing is hid from its heat. (Psalm 19:7)

And so we see: By virtue of such a comparison, which removes from God all that could not apply to God, we are transported into another region, in which Being is utterly different. God and things stand infinitely apart. It would seem that the bond that links them ought to burst. But when we reverse this perspective, by another comparison, in which negation continues to function, God is discovered to be, on the contrary, utterly near all things. God and created things—an abyss separates them, and yet without there being any distance between them.

10

God, Ever Utterly Near

When God arouses a new reality, first, He acts not "upon" things–or "against" them (as we are obliged to do)–but "in" them.

—Dom Vermeil

W E NOTICE THAT the contemplative quoted in the present epigraph also asks the "negative way" to lead him into the depths of the divine activity. In the preceding chapter, we have established that, in producing "being" in all things, God does not act as we do. God is transcendent to all things. God's activity is universal, like that of the sun. Now, we must also add, apropos of the divine activity, that God does not act as things do. God is immanent to each and every thing.

The corporeal substances of the world act "upon" one another. They remain, in their interaction, more or less external to one another. Even if the effects are interior, the causes remain exterior. The heat of the sun penetrates plants, but the sun itself remains at a distance. By contrast, in the divine activity itself, God, in the divine Being, is altogether intimately present to things!

We have seen that, of all of the effects of which God is the actual Cause, *existence* must be singled out. But existence gives to each thing its reality. It is existence that gives each thing the right to bear the name "being."

Thus, God resides immediately at the heart of things. St. Thomas pronounces powerful words:

> As long as a thing possesses being, God must be present to it, and this in the manner in which it possesses existence. Now, existence, in each thing, is what inheres in it most intimately and most profoundly. We may thus necessarily conclude that God is *in* all things, in an intimate manner. (*Summa Theologiae* I, q. 8, a. 1)

It is "necessary" that God be present at the core of the beings of this world, says St. Thomas. In order to become sensitive to this "demand" of the act of being, existence must cease to appear to us as a banal fact. The intellect must awaken to this act that is even deeper than the act of essence. The essence of natural beings is perceived to be at work in matter when it works there in order to thrust itself to the light. But existence is a different affair altogether. Existence is the force that "extracts" things from nothingness, from the abyss. One must "see" this—and it is like a miracle, says Maritain.[4] But to "see" existence for itself is not the exclusive privilege of the philosopher. Of a sudden, it can become an object of admiration for nonphilosophers as well. Ionesco, for example, writes: "What is behind and under the trappings? Incredible existence—'source of astonishment.'"[5]

Let us pause here. The verb "to be" usually denotes for us the presence of a thing before our eyes, as in the expression, "It *is* there, on the table." But without any phonetic or grammatical change, the same verb is charged with an actually metaphysical denotation. Then it denotes the *act* by which a thing emerges from nothingness. And suddenly the intellect discovers a new landscape, that of *being as being*. Suddenly the intellect sees that things, which *hold themselves* in their essences, are nevertheless *sustained*, maintained, held up above nothingness. And they cannot hold themselves above the abyss except

by the Being to which existence belongs per se! Then the verb
"to be" has finally spoken all of its "mystery"!

Its mystery is that this "act" in things implies the presence
of God in each thing, a presence utterly intimate, yet hidden
not only from the senses, but even from the intellect. A presence so intimate! As nothingness is nothing, there could not
be any intermediary between the thing that appears in existence and God who bears it above the abyss. This deed of God
is exercised toward all things and each of them. Therefore
God's immediate presence is called God's *presence of immensity*
to the world. And this presence is not merely enveloping but
also *penetrating*. Aristotle, who had seen the presence of God
as *Pure Act* moving each thing toward its end, had not seen this
other presence of God, now not only "enveloping" but "penetrating." And this Aristotle had not seen, because he had not
seen "existence" in its proper mystery!

To conclude this chapter, let us have a quotation from
Jacques Maritain. It will be relatively extended, but we shall
find it most enlightening.

> That God is *ipsum Esse subsistens,* subsistent Being itself, is the
> supreme, the most sacred metaphysical truth, seen by the
> "handmaid" [of theology, which is philosophy]—Saint Thomas's
> metaphysics, which has, if I may so speak, whispered it in the
> ear of his theology. But how comes it that Saint Thomas's meta-
> physics has seen this truth? Because God himself has told
> Moses, in the burning bush: "I am who am," and because it is
> in the fire of supernatural contemplation that the heart has
> meditated on the word spoken to Moses, and that the whole
> soul has burned with love for "the One who Is," that Saint
> Thomas has *recast* Aristotle's metaphysics in order to make of
> it a metaphysics founded in the intuition of being fully and for-
> mally possessed. . . . And this shows how philosophy can be
> reinforced and enhanced in its proper order, in being philoso-
> phy more than ever, and in better than ever accomplishing its
> work of *natural* wisdom, through faith and contemplation.[6]

11

God Immovable and Eternal

*You are immovable and eternal, Lord! As in the
beginning you have known the sky and the earth
without change of your knowledge, you have also
created, in the beginning, sky and earth without
your action passing through distinct steps.*

—St. Augustine

IT IS IN THESE TERMS that St. Augustine addresses God in
the *Confessions* (11.31). He is in ecstasy before these attributes of God. "O how great you are, and it is in the lowly of
heart that you dwell!" (ibid.).

With these attributes, of immovability and eternity, we once
more approach the divine Essence. We shall consider them
together: they hold hands, so to speak. We shall notice, furthermore, that St. Thomas makes use of the procedure of
negation. He approaches God by the *via negativa*.

When he speaks in the *Summa Theologiae* of the divine
immutability, St. Thomas observes:

Certain ancient philosophers, as if they had been forced by the
truth, have attributed immutability to the first principle of
things. Among these "ancient philosophers," the one who has
most strongly excluded all change from Being, is Parmenides,
who says, "Being is immobile, the prisoner of mighty chains,

55

without beginning and without end, since birth and death have been seen unthinkable for it. It abides without change in its being: the Immovable."[7]

Now, Parmenides is the first of the ancient philosophers to have regarded things from the angle of being. Furthermore, on the threshold of the temple of Wisdom, the goddess gives him this advice: "You must settle the problem by reasoning alone." But in thought, the idea of being, in itself, admits neither of having begun nor of ever being about to leave off: that would mean that, at a given moment, "being is not." That is a contradiction! And there you have it. In nature, in things, being presents itself otherwise. It has birth and death. It presents itself with other attributes!

Aristotle reproaches Parmenides with having failed to observe nature (*Physics* 1.8.33–34). It is first of all in the world of things that are born and die that our first encounter occurs with the act of being. Now, we have shown in part 1: it is sensible, temporal, and changing things that *demand* of spirit that it explain their being by way of the per-se-subsistent-immovable-Being. The existence of God is not a postulate of pure reason; it is things that call for it. Paradoxically, it is actually the fact of change of being in things that is the reason for the necessity of Pure Act.

In keeping with St. Thomas's method, we shall remove from the Essence of God what fits only the being of things. We shall remove from God all "passage": that from nothingness to being, that of matter to form, and all "accidental" change. ("Accidental": real but not sustantial, as with, for example, the weight of a thing, which is real but is not the thing itself). True, numerous propositions—especially those of the Bible—use verbs and nouns of God that denote movement: "God descends," "God ascends," "God inclines his ear," and so on.

St. Thomas Aquinas explains this language:

> "Approaching" and "withdrawing" are acts attributed to God by Scripture; but it is a matter of metaphor. We also say that the sun enters the house or leaves it, according to the presence of its rays. Just so, we say of God that he approaches or withdraws from us according to whether we receive the influence of his goodness or are deprived of it. (*Summa Theologiae* Ia, q. 9, a. 1, ad 3)

In conclusion: The attribute of "immobility" places God as far above the things of this world as the sun is higher than the earth. And yet, in the preceding chapter, we have had to say that the gift of God that is existence, bestowed on each thing, renders God so intimately present to each thing. Yes, God makes each thing to exist without this activity changing anything in him or affecting him in any way. Thus, one must never separate God's *immanence and transcendence* in speaking of God's relationship to the world and the world's to God. Unless these two modes of acting are held together when one speaks of God, we fall either into deism, for which God is far from the world and indifferent to it, or into pantheism, which confuses God and the world: two fatal errors to avoid in speaking of God!

Let us now speak of God's eternity. When we speak of God's being and acting, we ought never to use the words "before" and "after." In God's action there is no succession. Let us admit that it is very difficult to adhere to a rule like this, as we begin by encountering things that are in time. In order to understand why—once it is a matter of God in himself and his action in itself—we cannot extend the category of time up as far as God, we must define time. Now, time, both its notion and its reality, is a difficult thing to pinpoint. St. Augustine permitted himself a delightful turn of thought on the subject: "What is time? If no one asks me, I know; but if someone asks me and I want to explain it, I no longer know" (*Confessions* 11.14).

Time has two sources. The first is the movement in the being of material things, all of which have a "successive duration." For example, the duration of a plant is the totality of the changes that, from seed to blossom, succeed one another but without discontinuity. The other source is found in the human soul. Endowed as it is with memory, it can retain within itself a past fact when that fact no longer exists in reality. And because it is also endowed with an imagination, it can project into the future a fact that does not yet exist. And as our intelligence is the faculty that sets things in reciprocal relationship, it will join these two events by using the terms "before" and "after." In so speaking, we conform ourselves to the moving reality of the things of this world. Then the soul reaches toward what is no longer and what is not yet. It is the reflection in the human soul of the "distention" of things in themselves. St. Augustine sees in this the poverty of being that one finds in things. Being is "distended" between two "nothingnesses." "I see that time is a kind of distention. But a distention of what? I do not exactly know. Probably a distention of the soul itself" (*Confessions* 11.26).

Now a poverty of this kind could not be found in the Being of God such as it has appeared to us at the termination of the five ways that end in God. And so we must remove temporality from God's essence and activity alike. God's attribute is eternity.

God has never begun. God will never end. The *via negativa*, the way of negation, bestows on us a perfectly adjusted view. Temporality is found in the things that God makes; it is not found in the One who makes them.

When we say that God is eternal, it is from God and the divine activity whence we remove temporality, not from things. We cannot escape passing by way of this ignorance. In attributing eternity to God, we mean that God is not, and acts not, as natural things are and act. It is an avowal of ignorance that knows that it does not know. It is a *docta ignorantia,* a wise, a well-instructed ignorance. Claudel's expression is felicitous: "In that I know not, I come to know Him." Then an intelligence that consents to pass by way of this *via negativa* approaches God *really.* Only we must add at once what St. Thomas says: "We know that what we remove from Him we remove by reason not of a lack, but of an excess of perfection" (*Summa Theologiae* Ia, q. 12, a. 12).

From a knowledge of the poverty of being in the things of nature, in our part 1, we moved to the affirmation of the existence of God. Our part 2 contains especially an avowal of the poverty of our knowledge of the Essence of God. This poverty, which appears in our use of negations, paradoxically enables us to approach God's Essence as nearly as possible. Divine poverty!

12

One God, the One Orderer of All Things

*Everything **holds** in God: those who live in God never lack the fruit of their works. Works that leave us and return in their time in magnificent ordering.*

—Paul Claudel

BEING, THE FIRST CAUSE of existence in all things, a cause higher than the sun, a Cause unique! Only per-se-subsistent-Being can give being. There could not be several gods, says St. Thomas, finally, removing all multiplicity from God. Taking its position very precisely on the plane of the act of being, philosophical reason can easily demonstrate the unicity of God:

If there were more than one God, they should have to differ in something. Something would be attributable to one that would not be attributable to another. If this were the case, some perfection would be lacking to one or the other among them. And the one that this privation would affect would not be absolutely perfect. (*Summa Theologiae* I, q. 11, a. 3)

And thus would not be God!

60

By way of a buttressing argument, St. Thomas adduces the fact that "the ancient philosophers themselves, as if compelled by the truth, have asserted that the [concrete] principle of all things is unique" (ibid.).

The perfect possession of the Act of being is incompatible with privation of being. The ancient philosopher that St. Thomas has most in mind is Parmenides, who, speaking of being, said: "The being one is indivisible, because it is entirely identical with itself. Nowhere is it more dense: its cohesion prevents this. Nor is it anywhere more light. It is altogether filled with being."[8]

Meanwhile, there is another reason for the unicity of absolute Being that Parmenides has not seen. With Parmenides, the unicity of God is such that it excludes a multiplicity of things. There is no room for other beings. Still, as Aristotle says of him, "it would have sufficed to observe nature to dissipate his scorn. He has not seen that each thing in nature—this rose, this bird—works at its being. He has not seen—befogged as he has been by his reasonings—what a thrust grasps things at the moment of their generation, with what eagerness they are borne toward their ends, where they burst forth in colors, or in song! He has not seen that all of this order, that rules in the individual things of nature and among them, calls for a unique orderer: "After all," says Saint Thomas, "the oneness of order is better realized by the one than by the many" (*Summa Theologiae* I, q. 11, a. 3).

The teeming population of things is not anarchy. If this region in which being is multiple has been given the name of "cosmos," the Greek word for "order," it is because a certain oneness reigns among things:

All beings are mutually ordered. We see that certain things are at the service of others. Now things, different in themselves, would not concur to constitute a single order except by [the ordering of] a single orderer." Indeed, a multitude is subjected to a single order by a single one better than by a plurality. It is necessary, then, that the "first orderer" of all beings, according to an order that is single, be itself one. And this orderer is God. (*Summa Theologiae* I, q. 11, a. 3)

The oneness of God in the sense of uniqueness is another attribute that philosophical intelligence contemplates in God. It does so by denying of God any multiplicity—that is, by the *via negativa* once more!

Conclusion

*What, then, is God? I questioned the earth and all
that is to be found there. . . . I questioned the sea
and its abysses, and the living beings that move
there, and they answered me: ". . . We are not your
God. Search above us."*

—St. Augustine

IN THIS PART TWO, we have tried to express the Essence
of God by denying of God that which, in creatures, cannot
fit God. This is the manner proposed by St. Thomas for
regarding, above creatures, the hidden God. "Remove from
Him what in us could not fit Him." St. Augustine cries out to
God, "By comparison with you, things have neither beauty,
nor goodness, nor existence" (*Confessions* 11.4). If we should
now present a bouquet of the attributes that the *via negativa*
has enabled us to discover, here, in a few lines, is how it could
be made up.

God is a single, eternal, immovable substance. Never has
this substance begun, nor ever will it cease its act of being.
Nor has it had to compose its being. It is, so to speak, in an
eternal instant, in a bolt of lightning that lasts forever, that it
possesses its being. In it not the least shadow of a change
occurs. How easy it is to understand that such a Being can
communicate existence! The negations of which we have had

63

to make use in order to express its Essence are like a cloud, deep within which it hides its existence, its presence, its action. It is from this mystery that God emerges in order to enter into a relationship with the "teeming population of beings." St. Augustine prays:

> You have already said, Lord, with a strong voice in the ear of my soul, that you are eternal, that you alone have immortality. For you change neither in form nor in movement, and your will does not vary according to moments, a changing will not being immortal. This truth is clear for me in your presence. Grant, I beseech you, that it may become clearer and clearer to me, and that, in the shelter of your wings, I may wisely persevere in this evidence. (*Confessions* 12.11)

Part 3

Introduction

I N PART 2, IN ORDER TO KNOW the Essence of God, we asked things to fade away in some way before that Essence, to be able to utter it. We asked them to say of God what God is not, by saying that God is nothing of what they are. Nothing of what they are or of what we are is attributable as such to God. God does not compose his being, as things and we ourselves are obliged to do. Then, when their being and ours are achieved, we act on other things, but from without, and on few things indeed. *By contrast, per-se-subsistent-Being communicates to each thing that which is most intimate and most deep within it: being, existence.* In a word, we asked things, in denying themselves, to exalt the Being and Acting of God.

Now, here, after this effacement, we ask them, these same things, to lend us the names that fit God. But we must be careful! The names we borrow from them will never explain the divine Essence in itself. We concluded to the existence of God in part 1, giving God names that drew him out of our material and contingent universe. We have called him Pure Act, First Cause, Self-subsistent Being, Absolute Perfection, and First Intelligence. But these names placed his Essence beyond our grasp. And here we are having recourse to things in asking of them a positive service. The reason is that they are "effects" of God. As we know, all knowledge occurs by way of a likeness of the thing in the knower. Now, the things of this world are God's effects. And effects always resemble their cause in some aspects. Can we not use things—that is, these effects—in order to know and to name God on their basis?

True, what we know of God in this way is what created things return to us as from a mirror. Consequently, the names that we shall give God are names that are valid first of all for our world. But by way of some adaptations, we shall be able to attribute them to God. Our first question, then, will be the following. What is it in things that will be able to play the role of likeness to the divine perfection? Or again, what are the concrete perfections in things that can be found in God?

13

How Can Certain Perfections Be Found Both in Things and in God?

All of the great words are synonymous, or tend to become such. Order, unity, truth, goodness . . . they are constructed in a pyramid.

—C.-F. Ramuz

IF WE CAN ATTRIBUTE to God concrete perfections that are also in things, we must begin at the beginning and say that they are not in God according to the same mode of existence. Let us hear St. Thomas on this point.

> With regard to the names applied to God, two things are to be considered: the actual perfections that are expressed, as goodness, life, and the others, and the manner in which they are signified. As to the perfections themselves, these words that denote them can be said of God and of things in their proper sense, and of God in an even more proper sense than of creatures. It is to God that they are primarily applicable. But when we speak of the manner of signifying them, these same words no longer apply primarily to God. For the manner of signifying is the one that belongs first of all to the creature. (*Summa Theologiae* I, q. 13, a. 3)

69

Certain perfections are attributed to God, but on one condition: that they not necessarily imply imperfection. Hence they are called "pure perfections." We mean such perfections as do not "necessarily involve any imperfection in their notion."[1] But how are they to be found? We find them where they are said of the most diverse things. For example, being is a perfection attributed to a grain of sand, a flower, an animal, a person. It is a perfection capable of ascending through all categories. We see that it does not shatter on any of them. On the contrary, it is all the more true as we ascend the various categories. I already suspect that nothing will prevent its passing beyond the world. I understand what St. Thomas says: that this perfection will be attributable to God in the proper sense, and "with more justice than to the various creatures" (*Summa Theologiae* I, q. 13, a. 3).

Such is the case with being, and with all of the perfections that necessarily accompany being.

Let us take another example: the unity that always accompanies being. If a thing is not one, at least with a oneness of "composition," then it is not. This perfection actually ascends through all categories. It is a "pure perfection." Truth, goodness, beauty, are such perfections. They are said of all things. When Plato speaks of beauty in the *Symposium,* he begins by inquiring how and to what we attribute this perfection. And he sees that this perfection is said of bodies but also of spirits, souls, and their activities. It is an "oceanic" perfection.

The same is to be said of the perfections truth, goodness, and life, as also of cause and substance. Then we see that nothing prevents our saying these things of God. And one sees already that these perfections will be said of God primarily. But if I say that God is one, that God is true, good, beautiful, cause, and substance, I have to say that God is *all of this according to a superior, supereminent mode of existence.* I have found these perfections first in corporeal things. But they are there as if in exile! Charles Journet writes:

It will be the exclusive privilege of pure or absolute perfections, that is, perfections whose notion does not necessarily imply any imperfection, to be able—but in traversing a kind of death—to pass beyond the "as if" and the curtain of exterior behaviors, to signify directly what God is properly and truly: what he is in himself.[2]

14

Transcendental and Analogous Perfections

Over the lakes, over the valleys, the mountains, the forests, the clouds, the seas–beyond the sun, beyond the lakes, beyond the confines of the starry spheres, you, my mind, my spirit, move with such agility.
—Charles Baudelaire

THE PERFECTIONS OF WHICH we have spoken in the preceding chater are also called "transcendentals" and "analogous perfections." Why? The word "transcendental" comes from the Latin, and means "across" (*trans-*) and "climb" (*scend-*). We have seen these perfections span the rungs of the ladder of being to the very tip. "Beauty" is a "transcendental" because it is said of a precious stone, of a drop of dew sparkling in the sun, of a daisy that bursts forth white amidst the green grass, of the swallow that, in the evening, creases the blue sky, and we could continue until this perfection passes beyond this world into the divine. We feel in advance that it will not burst, because no category here below has been able to exclude it. So why should it stop? It is the same, to take another example, with the word "cause." I say it of all sorts of different things. The sun "causes" light; the rain "causes" freshness; the flower "causes" the beauty of the countryside; the intelligence "causes" science. I feel in advance that this word, too, can be employed to denote a relation of dependency beyond our world. Such perfections are called "transcendentals." Now we understand why.

They are also called "analogous." The word "analogous" comes from the Greek *ana*, "upwards," and *logos*, "reason." The word "analogical" denotes the movement of reason in tracing the transcendental perfections as they ascend through all created categories to God. "Transcendental" and "analogous," or "analogical," then, are interrelated concepts. For it is reason alone, that is, the intellect, that can follow such perfections, in mounting the categories just as do they. How can we see the degrees of being to their highest point? The eyes of the body cannot see above the "bodily." But then we must pose a new question: What makes a perfection incapable of being "shut up" in a species or kind, so that it transcends all of them instead?

The perfections called "transcendentals" have each the property of being constituted by a relationship. In these perfections, there are but two terms. These perfections can vary infinitely, according to different proportions. Being is constituted by reference of essence to existence. Truth is constituted by reference of being to the intellect. Goodness is constituted by reference of being to the will, to the rational appetite. Cause is constituted by reference to a dependency of one being on another being. The intellect, which is the faculty of reference and relationship, sees that such perfections can take on a multitude of modes. In music, for example, one can vary the relationship of two notes and draw from them a whole architecture of sound without ever destroying those two notes. As we see, the likeness on which we base ourselves in order to ascend to God is a perfection neither specific nor generic, but analogous, and analogous in similar proportions. This is what an analogous likeness or resemblance is. It is constituted by the relationship between two terms, whose proportions can infinitely vary.[3]

15

Reason's Triple Leap in Its Ascent to God

Happy the one who can vigorously soar toward the shining, serene fields.

—Charles Baudelaire

BAUDELAIRE HAS COMPARED human reason, in its ascent to God, to the flight of the lark. We have spoken too abstractly up to this point of analogous and transcendental perfections.

There is no escaping Baudelaire's comparison. Reason, that is, intelligence in motion, traverses all sorts and kinds of things by these analogous and transcendental concepts. The faculty of naming, which defines our species, signifies concepts first, not things. Aristotle insists on this. Now, in following thought in its leap to God, we notice that it makes, as it were, three bounds. In order to soar, the lark attempts it several times, pausing briefly each time. And we count, in the movement of reason toward God, three pauses, three leaps.

First, there is the leap of *causality*. These perfections linked to being are seen by the intellect to exist first in God, because it is God who is their First Cause. The intellect sees that it is in God that they have their proper existence. If the intellect sends them beyond the confines of this world, it is because it has seen that, here below, these perfections can be found only by way of participation—thus, received and therefore caused. Now, as if by instinct, the intellect departs for another world in search of this First Cause. For reason knows in advance that, in this material world, these attributes can be only participated.

And this brings us to the second leap, that of *negation.* The intellect concludes that, in this Being-Cause, these perfections will have a different mode of existence from the one they have in "things." And so the intellect denies that they are in God as they are in the things of this world.

Finally there will be the leap of *supereminence.* To deny a mode of existence is not to deny existence. The metaphysics of the pure perfections discovered here below does not know how they are found in God. It does know that they have in God their native country.

The human intellect as human admits that it does not know the mode of existence that these perfections have in God. But to admit that it does not know this mode is the part of *docta ignorantia,* "instructed ignorance." For the intellect knows that they are in God according to a supereminent mode (Thomas Aquinas, *De Potentia* q. 7, a. 5, ad 13).

And there we have three leaps. The last escorts the mind into ignorance. The human intellect, as human, can know a reality only by way of the senses, and to pass by way of the senses is ultimately to enter the divine darkness. This is a homage rendered to God: in a sense, one could say that this is the prayer of the metaphysician. And one could say, in this sense (as André Fossard writes), that Aristotle serves as acolyte at St. Thomas Aquinas's mass.

16

Participation in the Same Perfection

You see this person I am, and this being that I
take in you—O my God, my being sighs for yours!
                                                   —Paul Claudel

A PURE PERFECTION—one that has no limit in itself, tends toward God, in whom resides its pattern or exemplar. It has a kinship with God. Nor does this kinship come only from a resemblance. It also comes from a dependence. Even in the biological realm we are related, because we have a dependency on our ancestors. And it is because we depend on them that we bear the same name as they.

The case is the same with regard to God for all creatures, which all depend on God. If we give to certain things the same name as to God, it is because they all depend on God. We give them the name "being." Now, not only is there no reason why we should not, but, on the contrary, everything demands that being have an absolute existence somewhere. With reference to these perfections that are not limited in themselves, we can adopt an image of Jacques Maritain: "It is as if one plunged into the ocean, to find on its floor a magic mirror in which the sky were reflected."[4]

Since God's first effect in all things is existence, God is justly called the "per se existing Being." But it is with all justice as well that God has the name of the perfections necessarily bound to being. It can happen that we give several things (here below) the same name because there is a cause-and-effect relation between them with regard to the same perfection. For example, we call a climate "healthy" not because it has health within it formally but because it fosters that state. All the more shall we give things the name "being," because God is the Being-in-himself, and because, among things, being is the first of his effects.

We see, then, that a given perfection is "participated" in the things in which it resides along with other perfections. But nothing militates against there being a fuller realization elsewhere than here below. Indeed, everything demands it. By reflecting that this perfection was not yesterday and that tomorrow it will be no longer, we see that it is not in its native country. And we see that, being participated, it is received and hence caused. It is in its cause, then, God, on whom it depends, that this perfection is found in the pure state without any limit.

17

Great Poetry Is Invited to Speak of God

The most remote comparisons are the closest to the truth. They give us to understand that God is above all that we can say of him.

—St. Thomas Aquinas

WE HAVE BLOCKED the passage to the domain of God of the names that signify a specific or generic perfection in things. We have barred this route to them. And yet, how many words all charged with earth do take the heavenly path! Granted, therefore, along the biblical route God is given names such as Rock, Rampart, or Shield. It will be said that God has hands, eyes, ears. He is given names such as "eagle" and "lion." God is said to inhale the blood of sacrifices. We hear of his wrath, jealousy, the tenderness of his bowels, his heart. How are we to explain that these names predicate of God perfections that cannot be found in him formally?

Our astonishment would mean we have no understanding of the poets. We should have to know nothing of the gift possessed by certain human beings of, precisely, finding a kinship between things sometimes very removed from one another. We should have to be ignorant of the marvelous relationships that each thing has with another and even several others. We should have to be ignorant of what a great poet has said:

> Nature is a temple, in which living pillars
> at times permit the emergence of confused words:
> The human being passes there amidst forests of symbols
> that observe him with familiar glances.[5]

Astonishment at this power would be failure to recognize the need of the human being to cast upon the world the net of an "immense analogy" between the world of bodies and that of souls.

> Human being, forever shall you cherish the sea!
> The sea is your mirror—and you shall contemplate your soul
> In the everlasting heaving of its wave,
> And your spirit is over an abyss no less bitter.[6]

The authors of the Bible have received this marvelous power and have raised to God these names, once more, all charged with earth. To be sure, it will be necessary to interpret this language. But to begin with, one understands that in such a language there are comparisons, and that these words are *metaphors*. This term is composed of the Greek *meta*, meaning "beyond," and *phora*, a "carrying." Thus, a metaphor is a carrying of words beyond their native signification. Not only are these words great; they are too great. In their native usage, they were not destined to pierce the curtain of material perfections. But the poet obliges them to climb higher. And this is because "symbolic intelligence" is precisely suited for seizing relationships between earth and heaven at first unsuspected. The poetic intellect has wings. It carries these names beyond themselves. Thus, a poet sees relationships among things that an ordinary human being fails to see. For example, a poet writes apropos of a cypress:

> Like a shepherd in the mist,
> Counting his sheep and counting again,
> Anguish in his heart
> Under his narrow cape.[7]

For this stanza to be born, it has surely been necessary, be
it only in a flash, for this remote kinship to make its appearance, and for their similarity, for an instant, to be revealed. Let
us reflect on this unexpected rapport. The shepherd and the
cypress certainly do not possess the same nature. But in the
mist, immobile, his mantle tight, the shepherd resembles a
cypress. And suddenly the fire of intuition gathers them
together. Their resemblance "assembles" the beings. Biblical
poetry is made of these correspondences among things, or
between human beings and God. It is expressed by the route
of an intelligence eager to seize upon the traces of God in the
things he has created. St. John of the Cross asks things:

> O forests and woods,
> planted by the hand of the beloved bridegroom,
> O heath of verdure,
> of enameled blossoms,
> say whether he has passed your way![8]

And the saint himself comments on his poem, saying: "God,
who has made all creatures in an instant, with a great facility,
has left in them a reflection of his being."[9]

It is only too evident that there is no similarity between the
Essence of God and the realities here invoked! How is God literally like a rock? Only very remotely. Still, the Psalmist, who
lives in God, experiences at the bottom of his heart a peace so
profound as to be comparable to the sensation of security on
the part of a person who clings to a rock amidst a tempest, or
who hides in a hut during a storm. These rapports of kinship,
external as they may be, suffice to raise the name of "Rock"
and the name of "Hut" to God. To refuse the intellect this
route of poetic intuition would be, in a way, to suppress the
Bible. God has willed that the poetic intellect serve him sump-
tuously, by endowing our human words with a spring that carries them off to the regions where he is hidden.

18

Contemplation of Existence

What . . . Giacometti seeks to represent is
the mysterious act by which things rise up in
being before falling back just as quickly into
nothingness.

—Yves Bonnefoy

EXISTENCE IS ORDINARILY hidden from us by the appearances of things, and even by their essence. But especially, appearances veil it when they are beautiful and attractive, so that they cause us to tarry with them. Many painters have been satisfied with celebrating appearances. Often, this pleases us. Still, it is even better to see them abandon appearances and move toward essence. Can they go all the way to existence?

We are beholden to Cézanne for moving toward what there is in things, and their intimate structure or essence. Jacques Maritain pays homage to him by saying that what Cézanne shows is the "architectural authority with which things 'exist.'"[10] Now, Giacometti, for his part, was fascinated by another perfection found at the heart of things: existence. Yves Bonnefoy has said it with profundity of insight. He was fascinated "by the mysterious act by which things rise up in being before falling back just as quickly into nothingness." This time it is a matter of existence, at the heart of being. This explains his depriving things of their appearances, but going further. Passing over the habitual data of space, he increases the size of the human being out of all proportion. He thereby seeks to communicate to us what he himself has seen in things: the mystery of their *presence*, or what amounts to the same thing, the mystery of their *existence*.

After idealism, which left "things" out of consideration, by a violent act if not one of contempt for consciousness, or at least of a breach with the same, philosophers who are visited by the intuition of being have attempted to find it along a path other than that of pure intellect. Heidegger seeks it by the philosophical analysis of moods. He emphasizes a basic mood of the everyday: "Indifference and equilibrium, persistent and gray, mingled with disgust and ennui—and so we see that being is manifested as a burden; the being-there [the human being] sketches the being that reveals to him his mood."[11]

A whole current philosophy is devoted to the search for existence by first of all bracketing it. Other philosophers are impatient to find it again.

It will not do to bracket it. It enters into every perception—disguised, it is true, by the abundance of phenomena, and even by the essence in which it is always immediately deployed. Therefore it falls, with all of the rest of perfection or attribution. However, existence is the only perfection that can raise the intellect directly to God. The other perfections, notably essence, lift it to God only obliquely.

The contemplation of *existence*, we see, is the rarest thing, and yet the most necessary for our intellectual hunger. It is not, like essence, the force that organizes and directs matter, and lifts it architecturally into the light, as the rose. It is the most common and the most hidden. It is the force that lifts things out of nothingness. To discover this energy, this first energy—this "intelligible" at the heart of things—is the exclusive attainment of the person of biblical revelation. Even Parmenides, Plato, and Aristotle have not seen it. They have only approached it. In itself, however, it is an object of philosophy. And yet the greatest philosophers have not discovered it! St. Thomas writes: "On certain occasions, by grace, God instructs, miraculously, certain persons on truths that natural reason can know. Just so, at times, God produces miraculously certain effects that nature can realize" (*Summa Theologiae* I–IIae, q. 109, a. 1).

And this is the case with existence! St. Thomas tells us that God is the only one to cause existence. This activity of God's is called "creation." But how can we make existence to "appear" in a thing?

How may we render "sensible" that which is only intelligible, what an animal cannot see? Let us begin by observing that it is the very first act that it is given to each thing to realize. Before thinking and willing, a person must exercise the act of existing. Before a bird can perform the act of flying, it must be given the act of existing. And so on for everything. Now, this rose—and all of the things of nature with it—has nothing in it that could pretend to necessary existence, since it did not exist yesterday. Everything, then, admits this first poverty! It is what is called their "contingency." But it is also their "miracle."

It is significant, on this subject, that certain painters—and this is the case with Giacometti—having caught a glimpse of this act of "existing," and having sought to hand their vision on, have removed matter from their representation and have sought to remove it as much as possible. This is what explains the lengthened, threadlike figures of Giacometti. But they cannot do so completely without taking leave of the necessary means of their art. This perfection, existence, is known purely and in its proper mystery only by the intelligence, and then only when carried to the third degree of abstraction. The artists who have perceived it struggle in vain to give us an idea of it.

We must now explain how this perfection enables us to name God with his proper name.

19

The Name: Is "The One Who Is" the Most Proper Name of God?

If . . . they ask me, "What is his name?" what shall I say to them? God said to Moses, "I am who I am."

—Exodus 3:13–14

EXEGETES ARE AFRAID to give the name with which God named himself its philosophical meaning. They fear a reduction of revelation to the level of reason. And yet a great expert in Semitic languages has written: "This name, 'Yahweh,' could suggest the verb that in the old Israelite idiom denoted 'to exist,' 'to be.'"[12] It is possible for God to reveal even what, in itself, human reason could discover. Thus, we must give this expression its maximal force. It means: "The infinite Ocean of Substance."[13]

Taken in this sense, the expression is disquieting to philosophers. One of them observes:

A clear view of the phenomenon of being has often been obscured by a very general prejudice that we shall call "creationism." Inasmuch as it was supposed that God had given being to the world, being always appeared tainted with a cer-

tain passivity. But a creation *ex nihilo* cannot explain the rise of
being, for if being is conceived in a subjectivity, even a divine
subjectivity, it remains a mode of intrasubjective being. . . .
There could not be, in this subjectivity, even the representation
of an objectivity, and consequently it would be unable to be
affected by the will of creation of the objective.[14]

To this objection, St. Thomas responded in advance. God is
self-knowing, and, in this, God is subjectivity. But:

> If something is known perfectly, its power will necessarily be
> known perfectly. But the power of an agent cannot be known
> perfectly without a knowledge of the things to which this power
> extends. Just so, the power of God extends to "other" beings
> because God is the first efficient cause of all things. It is alto-
> gether necessary, then, that God know the "others." (*Summa
> Theologiae* Ia, q. 14, a. 5)

Further: God is not obliged to create. The only necessary
(while spontaneous) object of the divine love is God, the being
of God. All the rest, then, all that is not God, God can love
only freely. This is why we call it "gratuitous" when God gives
being to things "without rival contact." God's creation is not a
destructive contact. This is what God gave Moses to know in
appearing to him in the midst of a burning bush. But God
burns without consuming the bush of creatures, as well. A
great theologian has written:

> God is in the world like the fire in the bush, and he does not
> consume it. When God speaks to Moses in the midst of the
> fire, he reveals to him his most fundamental name, and mani-
> fests to him that being, which is present in all of the creatures
> in the universe, at the heart of even the humblest of creatures,
> is but a light veil that hides the splendor that is God's.[15]

What is so beautiful in this view is that it is on account of
the nothingness that each thing comes from, it is on account
of its total poverty, that, in order to communicate existence to

it, God is obliged in some way to approach it, to come to the remotest interior of each thing, for the being that is mine is even more God's than mine, inasmuch as I am a creature. This view, with all apologies to Sartre, reason could have known by itself. Yet God has miraculously instructed certain human beings in it: "All your children shall be taught by the Lord" (Isa. 54:13).

While God is intimately present to things, he is infinitely different from them. Our intellect is readily confused by the imagination. It ever runs the risk of confusing spatial distance with distinction in being. God is precisely the one who is infinitely close to each thing because God gives them what is most intimate in them: existence. But because God is the only one to be able to do this, he is infinitely distinct from each being. God is infinitely transcendent. Infinitely near, infinitely distinct.

God is the Ocean of being. God is the Ocean of strength, the Ocean of light always in act. The beings of the world do not emerge from nothingness without God's freely, gratuitously willing it so. In giving them the very first of perfections, existence, God thereby gives to each creature the power thus to realize its program in the world, which, for each one, is its fundamental thrust and its gladness!

But it remains to be explained how things are in God, in that luminous source of their being—that is, how God knows them.

Part 4

Introduction

I have a mystical love for natural reason.

                      —Raïssa Maritain

USING NATURAL REASON ALONE, we shall now attempt to say how it is that things, before being in themselves, are in God. In this precise area, we must retain a certain basic view: things do not precede the knowledge that God has of them, as they precede ours. God does not know them because they exist; they exist because God knows them. This is a truth that we shall have ever to keep in mind, throughout this part 4.

This view—that the knowledge of God "forms" things—is ceaselessly asserted by St. Augustine: "God does not know the universality of creatures corporeal and spiritual because they are. But they are because God knows them" (*De Trinitate* 15.13).

St. Thomas, for his part, will not leave off saying: "The knowledge of God is the cause of things" (*Summa Theologiae* I, q. 14, a. 8, ad 3).

Throughout this question, we must reverse our habitual manner of speaking and therefore speaking on the subject of the relationship of the world to God and vice versa. We commit many errors in this area. We almost always speak as if God's knowledge came to God from without. On the contrary, God's knowledge is creative, and thus anterior to things. God's knowledge is like the knowledge of artists with respect to their works. God does not draw from things the knowledge he has of them. Quite the contrary, it is from God's knowledge and God's love that they proceed. God's knowledge and love are the first source. This is things' nobility, but also their radical poverty. Each one could apply to itself the distych of Angelus Silesius:

> Born of God, I! The Spouse, in creating me,
> must needs leave me the nobility of Nothingness.[1]

The divine thought is in no wise measured by creatures. Just the opposite of this, God measures their being. This view finally gives us the ultimate reason for their dependency and their poverty. Like the work of art, they would not be, without this light and this tenderness that explain them in their depths. And the peace of knowing is great: "That soul is serene that measures its weakness," we can also read in the Cherubic Pilgrim.[2]

20

Things in God

*As God makes to exist, outside himself, created
participations of his essence, so the artist places
himself, and not what he sees, in what he makes.*
—Jacques Maritain

A S WE BEGIN THIS CHAPTER, we think that, in order to
say well what there is to say, we ought somehow to fuse a
metaphysician and an artist. Why? Because, apropos of the
world, it is difficult never to transfer our speculative knowledge to God. We mean, not to make of God the mirror that
reproduces things. Everything that exists, from the most general to the most particular, is certainly known by God. But
once more, it is known by him not because things exist, but in
order that they exist. This is the metaphysician's viewpoint, as
St. Augustine and St. Thomas never forget when they speak of
God's concrete reference to the world.

"In God, ideas precede things; they create them," says one
of their disciples, and he adds: "Therefore, in order to find
here below some analogy to these ideas, theologians compare
them to the ideas of the artist." But how difficult it is to hold
on to this truth, that in God the ideas he has of things proceed
not from them but from him! We are so accustomed to "per-
ceiving" in ourselves likenesses to things external to ourselves,

that we measure the knowledge of God on the pattern of our own, ordinary knowledge!

We are asking of our readers a complete turnabout in their thinking. On this point they shall have to substitute, for their habitual manner of speaking, a completely different language. They shall have to accustom themselves to seeing things as intermediaries between themselves and God. St. Thomas compares the knowledge God has of things to the knowledge of an architect: "Things are like a house, which is the intermediary between the knowledge of the architect who has built it and the knowledge of the one who presently sees it" (*Summa Theologiae* I, q. 14, a. 8).

The house exists first under the mode of an idea or plan, in the intellect of the architect. This is how God knows things. They would not exist unless God knew them. Actually, God first knows his Essence and almighty power. But God would not know his almighty power unless he also knew all of the things to which his power extends.

We must not fear to say it, then. When we contemplate a thing, we contemplate a work of God. But when we contemplate a work of Cézanne—for example, *The Sea at l'Estaque*—it is evident that this landscape, as such, exists only on the canvas that he has painted. It does not exist as such in reality, in the world. The painter does not intend to make a photographic image of this landscape, but a creation. What we see on the canvas is indeed this landscape, but, as it were, "transubstantiated" by the emotion and vision of the artist. Jacques Maritain, speaking of the labor of the artist, can write:

> Not only are things transfigured in passing from his eye to the hand. At the same time, another mystery is designed: the soul and the flesh of the painter strive to replace the objects he paints, removing the substance of the latter, entering and giv-

ing themselves in the appearances of these things, representing nothing in the world and shaped on the canvas, which live another life there than their own.[3]

When we look at a painting, we do not compare it to the things themselves that are outside the painter, in the world. We look at an ensemble of reversed signs, representing the painter's soul. As Malraux has said of van Gogh, his canvasses are "hieroglyphs" of his soul. One can say this more or less of every creator, every artist. A painting, a statue, a poem, a sonata, are first of all created, made things. They give us first of all to know the heart, the soul of their author.

In this same way, we shall be regarding things no longer in themselves, as does the scientific, speculative mind. We shall be contemplating them as signifying to us the divine Essence in which they have originally existed as ideas. Claudel reports to us what Mallarmé said: "What I contribute in literature is that I do not place myself before a spectacle and say, 'What is this?' and try my best to describe it, but I say: 'What does that mean?'"[4]

21

How Does God's Knowledge Open Out to Things?

All sources are in you.

—Raïssa Maritain

IT IS IMPOSSIBLE to exaggerate the wonder of Aristotle's explanation of God's self-knowledge. First he shows that God is unable to know anything but himself. As Père Sertillanges says, "There is in God nothing but God."[5] God cannot know anything but himself. Here is a passage from the great text in book L of the *Metaphysics,* where Aristotle says:

> The [concrete] principle of all things past is Life. We can compare this Life to the one given to us, but only for brief moments. God has this Life always. For us it is impossible. We must not even say that he "has" this Life; rather he *is* this Life. And this Life is for him a source of gladness. He is this gladness in act. With us, what causes us joy are acts, as of sensation and a thought. It is as acts that they are a source of rejoicing. . . .
>
> As for God, he is Thought per se. And he can only think what is the best for himself. Now, what is the best object that the divine Thought can have is himself, that is, his Thought. Thus, God is for himself the act of contemplation of perfect beatitude. And indeed the state of joy that his contemplation acquires for him, God always has, and this is admirable. (7.1072b.4–25)

What is Aristotle saying? God cannot have an object of knowledge other than himself. He is necessary because he is God, because he thinks what there is of the most divine. But who does not see that this knowledge seems to cut off all contact of the divine Thought with the world? God cannot change objects or have any object but himself. We can only conclude: God is Thought ever in act, which thinks eternally what there is of the most excellent, that is, itself.

It is St. Thomas Aquinas's stroke of genius to express the knowledge of the world that God must have in terms of the divine knowledge of which we have just been speaking. But this knowledge does not emerge from God toward things. It is things that "emerge from God."

It is because he knows his Essence perfectly, St. Thomas will say, that God also, and necessarily, knows things. Here is St. Thomas's argumentation.

> God knows himself perfectly. Now, of what is known perfectly, the power must be known. And it is impossible to know the power of a being perfectly without knowing the things to which this power extends. Inasmuch as it is certain that the divine power extends outside of God, since it is the first efficient cause of all things, it is absolutely necessary that God know other beings. (*Summa Theologiae* I, q. 14, a. 5)

And St. Thomas recalls that God has, with things and with respect to the divine knowledge, the relationship that artists have with their creation. Of Charles Baudelaire's *Le Confiteor de l'artiste,* which says, "All of these things think by me and I think by them,"[6] God could say, "All things preexist in me, as in their creative Cause. And it is as the artist that I bear them in myself, in a divine subjectivity. It is their grandeur, the grandeur of things, to be borne totally in the divine thought— but this grandeur is also their marvelous poverty."

22

How Are Things in God?

Not one breath of my life do I not borrow from
your eternity.

—Paul Claudel

"THERE IS NO ESSENCE because there is no God to think them."[7] The philosopher who makes this shattering declaration held implicitly, then, that if God exists, things have existed in God who has thought them. But how can one maintain that there are no essences? The facts themselves speak here and reply: Unless one is blind, how can one deny that things surely "compose" their being? They work at well-arranged organs that they "grow" at the same time. They assemble these organs, all of them well unified.

Things work at their organs a long time before using them. The swallow, for example, grows wings in the egg, when it would be unable to use them. In their constructive phase, things prepare themselves to have their role. They know their program in advance. They know, we might say, the instruments of which they will have need. Nevertheless, although they are capable of composing their being, and, to this end, of giving themselves so many things, they are incapable of giving themselves existence!

For example, a flower is to have the role of jonquil, a bird the role of blackbird. When I consider these beings growing from their seed, developing on the basis of that seed, in their egg, I see that they are busily preparing the tools of which they will have need for their program. Still, I see that they have not had "existence" in their program. Yesterday they did not exist. And tomorrow they will be no more. And yet we call them by the name of "essences."

The name of "essence" that the philosopher gives to things bespeaks the fact that they have an immediate concrete reference to existing. The word "essence" clearly announces that it comes from *esse*, which means "to exist." To call something an "essence" is to denominate its so profound concrete reference to existence. Once they have received it, how they cling to it! But—and this is paradoxical—nothing in this world is the proper owner of its existence, nor does it give itself existence, although existence is so precious and so necessary! And yet it is its dearest, most desirable good, its radical perfection (concrete attribute), its root. But then, who can give it? Who is its source? Is there a being with whom existence is its due? Is there a being that contains this perfection in itself and per se? Then it could give it. This would be a perfect being, a being full of being, in which nothingness would have no place. That being could grant existence as a gift. It would be the only being that could give other beings this perfection. Now, since things exist that do not have existence in themselves and per se, it follows that they have received it. And if they have received it, they do not have it per se, they "participate it."

Thus, it is in this being, and in this being alone, that things have been able to find their "reason" for existing. This is equivalent to saying that this being has allotted them their "ration" of existence (Latin *ratio*, "reason"). It is the Essence that has a reason to exist in and of itself, that can decide to what and how it will give existence.

In their capacity as realized outside the divine intellect, one can call them creative "ideas." The expression is borrowed entirely from the domain of art. It means that essences in God—all possible participations of the divine Essence—when God decides to realize them, are then called divine "ideas." These "ideas" are these essences capable of becoming, in things, the "forms" of construction, the forms of composition. Deposited in matter, they become operative; they work with matter to make a being. They are not, in things, ideas to be known, but ideas for being. And the essences in God that are realized in things are called, in respect of this realization, "ideas."

It is still the same doctrine. God does not know things because they exist, they exist because God knows them first. We see that all things depend on God in their being. It is their wealth, their poverty!

23

The Ultimate Perfection of Being: Subsistence

For it was you who formed my inward parts;
   you knit me together in my mother's womb. . . .
My frame was not hidden from you,
when I was being made in secret,
   intricately woven in the depths of the earth.
                  —Psalm 139:13–15

GOD'S ART DOES NOT STOP with species. In the world, we do not encounter a species as such, that is, a species in the abstract state. In fact, to speak of an "abstract thing" would be a contradiction in terms. God creates only individuals: this rose here, this titmouse there. A like observation could seem a banality, and yet it is an important piece of philosophy, the philosophy of the individual and the subject. Père Sertillanges makes the observation: "Intervening in the world of essences, the individual introduces a new and irreducible fact there."[8]

In the preceding chapter, we emphasized the fundamental aspiration of essences to existence. Now we are before another fact, that existence is given always and only to individuals. And thereby it gives us to recognize their price. For we grasp that, ephemeral as they are, these things receive the primordial gifts of essence and existence. But only God can give existence, and essence as such is first thought by him.

Now, the individual is also called to be a "subject," and to behave as a subject. We discover the whole depth of this word "subject" if we recall the sentence diagraming of our grammar-school days. To call something a "subject" was to place it at the head of a proposition. Martin Heidegger says that the subject, the individual, "marches at the head of being."[9] He means that, in the order of being, the subject is the very first perfection.

What we call a "subject" can very well enter into a relationship of knowledge or love with other subjects. But the main thing we mean in bestowing the name of "subject" upon a being is that this thing receives existence and essence and makes them its own—they belong to it. We call this thing "subject" because it first appropriates existence and essence and makes them its "own," refusing to allow their appropriation by another. Thus, it is created with the existence given to it. But it is not existence that makes it unique. Existence, as it happens, is per se communicable to all other things, to an indefinite number of individuals. Nor can we find in essence what renders a thing unique. That same essence is given to so many individual things. It is with another perfection of being that we must seek incommunicability, and thus the constitution of a "subject." This perfection is called "subsistence." The perfection of subsistence has immediately to do with existence, and, as it were, precedes it. It can only be created then, like existence.

In endowing it with subsistence, God renders existence incommunicable. I cannot say, "The existence is Peter." But I can say, "Peter exists." Now, God bestows this absolutely first perfection precisely in order that existence, and everything else, not be dissolved in him when he "supports" them for the continuation of their existence. It is in order that one thing among others may be able to enjoy it for its own sake, and thereby construct its program, that such a perfection is given it. We appreciate the blindness represented by Jean-Paul Sartre's reflection:

> One cannot conceive of a creation on condition that the created being regain itself, withdraw from the Creator, in order to close up in itself at once and assume its being. It is in this sense that a book exists "against" its author. But if the act of creation must continue indefinitely, if there is no actual independence, if there is nothing in itself but nothingness, then the creature is in no way distinct from its Creator—it is "resorbed" into him: we should be dealing with a false transcendence, and the Creator cannot even have the illusion of emerging from his subjectivity.[10]

Sartre's analyses actually show the need for subsistence. If God did not give each thing a subsistence, that is, the concrete principle that would give it existence as "its own," Sartre's remarks would have their pertinence. But the opposite is the case. Subsistence gives an individual precisely to be the subject of existence. It then becomes "its existence." God does not withdraw from things their individual existence at the moment that he gives each thing to make it its own. This would be absurd. It is true that the absurd, for this philosophy, is the last thing to be feared!

Let us say precisely the opposite. God shows us, on the level of a philosophical analysis, the benevolence residing in him. This benevolence flashes forth by the gift, each time, of existence, to a unique being. In the order of the existence and being of nature, the Creator, in giving each thing subsistence, in enveloping it with his activity, shows it that he loves it with a love common to all things, to be sure, but with a love, a choice, a gratuity, nonetheless, that already reveals what its value is in his eyes!

24

Relationship of the World to God and God to the World

> *We should see the world rise up in the unheard-of splendor of its Edenic nakedness, a rose, all fresh and transparent, made of relations to God.*
>
> —A Carthusian

CHAPTER 23 WILL HAVE GIVEN US to discover that, in the depths of things, perfections are found whose sole Cause and Bestower is God. The conclusion of that chapter was that subsistence, existence, and essence, in themselves, were ontological perfections, which means perfections constitutive of every being, of every act of being. But one who sees this, sees by that very fact that the world is suspended from God—sees that God is the Being of every being.

But now the delicate problem arises: How are we to express, how are we to define, the relationship that this world maintains with God? What is the relationship of the world to God?

We are presented with two extreme positions. Some think that, if God is the immediate cause and the preserver of all of the being of things, of every act of being, these things go up in smoke, to be dissolved in God. Thus, for the being of things to receive nothing from God, being must be first of all opaque, massive, uncreated, having no rapport with God. A relationship of dependence on God would, we are told, be dangerous for the consistency of the world. The world would be absorbed by God. It would lose its being. And so these thinkers deprive things of any relation to the ontological ladder. Things fail to enter into relationship with the human being, a relationship of knowledge, of service. But before the intervention of the human being, the being of things presents itself as an inert block, to which the human being gives its first form. But before the intervention of the person, being would be the being that has nothing. Being would be a nothingness of essence. We hear the echoes of the shattering declarations of Jean-Paul Sartre, who says that things have no essences because there is no God to think them. We have already said what is to be thought of this assertion.

Conversely, certain philosophers, in order to analyze relations between the world and God, have posited a God who changes. Here is what Maritain says on the subject of Hegel.

> God is immanent to the becoming of things. God and they are Thought, univocally. It is himself that he denies and rediscovers in the engendering of the universe, of time, and who, in the progress of history—the complete wealth of Spirit—is contained in each of the Worlds or historical Spirits, in the successive movement of human becoming. . . . Without the Calvary of history, the mind would be solitude without life.[11]

We reject this view of God. We have shown how and why God is beyond becoming and multiplicity—the First Intellect, Pure Act, the per-se-subsistent Being. No, the relationship of God to the world and the world to God must be conceived otherwise.

But having come to this point, we must refine the concept of "relation." First, we must observe that, between God and the world, relations are "relations of reason," relations only in our way of looking at things, while relations between the world and God are real relations. What do we mean by this? Let us consider an example in the area of knowledge. We are not forgetting that it is by an act of the divine Intellect that the world will come into being. This daisy in the meadow, which has attracted my attention by its white-and-gold flash in the green of the grass, gives rise to a "relation" of knowledge. Now, the knowledge that I receive from it does not change it. Nothing has shifted in it because I know it—not the least "twitch." And yet this knowledge initiates a "relation" between it and myself. And nothing has changed in the being of the daisy. And it is a good thing that this is the case. If the daisy underwent a change in its being every time it is known—and this can be thousands of times—how would it be able to offer the same joy to thousands of subjects of consciousness? But a relation of this kind changes nothing in the daisy. The "relation" between myself and the daisy is real; the relation between the daisy and myself is a relation of "reason"—that is, is only thought of as a relation, while in objective reality such a relation does not exist. The knower is actually changed. In his or her psychic reality, the subject is enriched by the being of the thing that has become an object within him or her. This subject is enriched, in the psychic order, with the being of the thing, in letting it be what it is. Such a relation gives us "to be more." While remaining the same thing, this blossom can take on a new mode of existence—an existence in the beholder—without suffering any change, without undergoing any alteration.

This is the case, analogously, in the order of God's creation. The relation begotten by the act of creation is real on the side of the world, while it is "of reason" on the side of God. What do we mean by this?

25

When the Philosopher Calls on Art to Suggest This Mysterious Relation

> ... *When I was being made in secret, intricately woven in the depths of the earth.*
>
> —Psalm 139:15

L ET US ANALYZE a concrete, visible example of the double relation that we here present. God's relation to the being of each thing does not have the dramatic character we see reflected in the Herculean Father on the ceiling of the Sistine Chapel, nor, again, the severe regard of the "Pantocrator" in the middle of the rose window of Beauvais, beautiful as they are! How can we translate "plastically" the sweet power of the creative act? The poet says: "I feel very palpably that this creation, that is but a collection of parables and meanings, is not capable of containing Him; on the contrary, it is He who contains it, suspended from three of his fingers."[12]

Perhaps Fra Filippo Lippi has succeeded in transmitting what we need to see in his *chef-d'oeuvre* of Berlin, *Nativity*. We see the Father bending tenderly over the plump little infant asleep in time. Three narrow rays of light emerge from heaven and descend on the infant. The whole atmosphere is one of the silence of all creation as it envelops all things. "While a deep silence envelops all things, . . ." says Wisdom. Aristotle, for his part, said, in the light of metaphysics, that "pure Act envelops all things" (*Physics*).

We could also use the image of the lover. But now we enter into the sphere of the final cause, "purpose cause," the cause by attraction. A theologian who is fond of this image writes: "God has, as it were, inhaled being up from nothingness. By breathing without moving. The *Divine Comedy* uses somewhat the same image, when Dante says, 'Love moves all things, by desire.' The beloved, magnetized, if you will, attracts her partner as if he had been iron filings, but without herself being in movement. She sets all aquiver, but without being in motion herself."[13]

The same theologian continues:

> We need two complementary images. We must say, simultaneously, that God's power is deployed in order to show the initiative of God, who makes the universe to appear; and then at the same time, in another image: God has inhaled, and behold, the world comes up from nothingness.[14]

Aristotle, too, admitted that an efficient cause (a thrusting cause, as opposed to an attracting, "final" cause) could give its act without being itself moved. He liked to give the example of the schoolteacher. "The teaching given is the same as that received." And he added:

> There is no reason why the same act should not belong to two different subjects. It is not necessary that the being that teaches "receive" the teaching—that is, that he change. The content of the teaching is the same with the pupil as with the master. But with the pupil, it is like that which is in presence, facing what is act. (*Physics* 3.202b.5–19)

And so, God, who is Being, gives being. God acquires noth-

ing, but gives all being. But God, Being-in-act, receives nothing. And St. Thomas puts on the finishing touch: "God alone
is absolutely generous, for he does not act for his own advantage, but only in view of his goodness, which is to make things
to participate in being" (*Summa Theologiae* I, q. 44, a. 1, ad 1).

General Conclusion

The mission of art is to find, in the world of the relative, the symbols [and proofs] of the absolute.

—Pierre Reverdy

WE SHOULD LIKE TO EVOKE the relations of a contingent world to the absolute and offer proof that the things of this world, regarded in a certain fashion, are the vessel of the proof of the Absolute. We should like, to this end, to yield the floor to poetry. We think that, sometimes—perhaps often—poetry is the vehicle of authentic metaphysical intuitions. Indeed, Saint-John Perse asks himself: "Between discursive thought and the poetic ellipse, which goes further, and comes from further?"[1]

And he adds, specifying the role of poetic thought:

> By analogical and symbolic thought, by the remote illumination of the mediating image, and by the play of its correspondences upon a thousand chains of foreign reactions and associations—finally, by the brace of a language in which the very movement of Being is transmitted—the poet dons a "surreality" that cannot belong to science.[2]

To bring our book to a conclusion, we offer a commentary on a poem by Anne Perrier. This poem, entitled, "A la Rose" (To the Rose) is certainly a poem on a relative reality that leads to the absolute. First, let us have the poem itself, in translation from the French:

111

I

Summer is no more . . .
Bled
The black ditch in the air
Trembles endlessly
O shattered time!
O day
Why name the rose
Since it must die
Words nod off
Too late . . . O rose to ignore you
Is no longer possible!
For ever between you and me
This bond this void
I have wept too much
Shall I see you when the rain is over
Will there be a morning
Will there be a summer
And will there be
At last my heart tranquil enough
To be the garden
Of your everlasting absence

II

If the world among a thousand thorns
Locks up its mystery
What is that to me?
But in this light
And this perfume both lost
My heart reels . . .
I have heard the silence crumple
O rose do you tremble
At knowing yourself deathless?
At knowing yourself perishable?

III

Peace my soul peace
The rose is but on a journey
Who could destroy it
And the universe not shudder?
Peace my soul peace
The rose is near regard
The shimmering of pain in the shadow
Do you see nothing?
It will be enough perhaps
That the bees stray

IV

Shall I speak to you long still
As to a death?
The birds on my table crackle
The hour leans through the window
And drinks the new weather, the new time
The angel is at the door

V

Rose O marvel
Shall I forever abide it
That you cheer me that you leave me
That at the instant in which you overwhelm me
You are already secretly lost
And that my heart of earth ever
Holds but your passage

VI

Who am I to understand
Your dazzling lesson

To follow you endlessly
On the slender slopes of day
My feet encircled with fear
And the cold of the abyss in my loins?
Me obscure little wanderer
Will you teach the sublime?

VII

Gleaming night
I shall go no further
It is here the road ends
It is here I shall sit down
That I shall await in peace
The time to pass the bank
Rose you cannot yourself
Lead me beyond the waters
Let us wait here
In dying you splash all the valley with flowers
I hide in your splendor
Today
May your mystery be enough for me.

VIII

Day will come I await him
I shall leap to meet him
I shall kiss his feet
I shall say lover to him
I shall lose myself in his jonquil heart
Shall I see then shall I see
The white rose-bush
Where slowly ripens
Your scarlet glory?

IX

Had you not passed under the wheels of time
Would you be she
Whose perfume intoxicates me
Whose one rare sweetness
Locks tight my sleep
Would you be blessed, happy
Among all roses
And clothed
In the flesh of the angels

X

Rose pure spilling
From heaven
On the paths you are to me
But the sign resplendent
Fleeting
Of the everlasting plenitude
You are beautiful
It is Beauty that I will have
Light up the universe and die
Pass into the shadow where I lose you
Leave the night under my eyes
Happy death happy night
Will you have led my soul
To the very walls of Paradise?[3]

In order to enter upon the explanation of this poem that
we propose, we must keep in mind what St. Thomas says of the
knowledge God has of individual things—of, if we may so
speak, "individual essences":

> As God knows other beings by the intermediary of his own
> Essence, inasmuch as this Essence is the similitude of things,
> or, again, their efficient principle [producing cause], it is nec-
> essary that his Essence suffice to make him know all of the

things that are made by him, and this not only in their universal nature, but in their singularity, as well. The case would be
the same with the knowledge of the artisan, if it produced the
entire thing instead of giving it only its form.

And a few lines further on, he adds the most important
thing: "It is from the essence of God that all of the constitutive principles of the thing proceed, including those of its specific nature and those of individuation. By his Essence, then,
God can know all individuals in this way" (*Summa Theologiae* I,
q. 14, a. 11).

Armed with St. Thomas's conclusion, we are now in a position to comment on this poem.

One summer's day a relation is struck between "this rose"
and the poet. Is this rose a symbol of beloved being?

> . . . O rose to ignore you
> Is no longer possible!
> For ever between you and me
> This bond this void
> I have wept too much . . .

This bond is born in summertime, in the light and heat of
a day. But autumn comes, with its rains. The weather changes
abruptly. The poet wonders:

> Will there be a morning
> Will there be a summer
> And will there be
> At last my heart tranquil enough
> To be the garden
> Of your everlasting absence

The poet knows that in order to rediscover "this rose," a
peaceful heart would be necessary and sufficient. And so she
addresses her soul. She will thus make the place of her indi-

vidual, but eternal, essence there. Hence the insistent appeal
to the soul.

> Peace my soul peace

The rose, or rather, "this rose," is the symbol not only of the
fragility of this world. But that it could have died—which is
impossible—proves that its essence is elsewhere: it is everlasting, in God. For it is in God that it was first formed and that
it is deathless!

> O rose do you tremble
> At knowing yourself deathless?
> At knowing yourself perishable?

The rose formed in God has served as a model for this rose,
born in time and already gone. But the one that is in God, and
is individual in God, as well, cannot have perished. The poet
knows this very well!

> Who could destroy it
> And the universe not shudder?

The pain of having lost it has drawn it closer. It is still visible, but in shadow. One must remove the obstacles to its
knowledge. But the poet has a presentiment that death alone
will restore it to her. Nor, for that matter, will death tarry.
Many an indication tells us that its hour approaches. For the
hour no longer ascends. It descends with the sun. It teeters
toward death. But the poet voices a complaint:

> Rose O marvel
> Shall I forever abide it
> That you cheer me that you leave me
> That at the instant in which you overwhelm me
> You are already secretly lost. . . .

God has taught the poet what the reasons are for every
being, especially for "her rose." But in order to enjoy this "daz-

zling lesson," one should have to inhabit the bottomless heart of God. But this rose cannot lead the poet to the banks of eternity.

> Rose you cannot yourself
> Lead me beyond the waters

This rose that has intoxicated the poet does not have the power, the strength of God. It is a creature, and consequently incapable of transporting the poet beyond the waters, into God's eternity, where "this rose" gleams immortal.

> Rose you cannot yourself
> Lead me beyond the waters

Let us pause here. In the night of this world. Time passes. Let us await the place, at last, where, in full light, the rose in its individual essence will be contemplated. For today, the poet hides in its splendor! She is profoundly moved.

> Shall I see then shall I see
> The white rose-bush
> Where slowly ripens
> Your scarlet glory?

But, in passing through time, the rose has suffered. For that matter, this is part of the reason it is so precious to me. But now it will don the flesh of the angels.

This beloved rose has appeared in time. Then it has departed. But thereby it has revealed to me that its individual model is in God, for it cannot die. And so it has passed here below as a fleeting sign.

> On the paths you are to me
> But the sign resplendent
> Fleeting
> Of the everlasting plenitude

Could we better end this book than with a song like that? The poet contemplates the same essence that dons mysteriously contrary liveries. One and the same "essence," once with its contingent existence, fleeting, and again with its eternal existence. This double existence is such that one is entirely relative to the other, because the one cannot be understood without the other. But who sees this? The metaphysician and the poet. The metaphysician and the poet "ride a teeter-totter, lifting each other to heaven by turns. The spectators make fun of them—the spectators seated on the earth."[4]

If, to end this book, we have commented on this poem, it is because the rose is surely the symbol of frail, fragile being. At the same time, could any reality bespeak, for us, better than the rose, the slow effort with which it labors at its essence? Is there any flower like it to recall for us that creatures' existence is precarious? Let us listen to another poet: "Ah! When we inhale this bouquet that makes the gods to live, it leads us only to this small, insubsistent heart that, if you take it with your fingers, sheds its petals and melts."[5]

Essence and existence—these are the two forces that build the being of each thing. St. Thomas Aquinas attributes all primacy to them. Essence manifests itself by its phenomena— by its activities and outward appearances. But existence is precisely veiled by the appearances that arrest the attention. Many painters have been content to celebrate appearances in things. They have represented them altogether felicitously. But in our century especially, we see them abandoning these appearances to turn to something beyond phenomena. It is to the essences of things that they are attracted. Cézanne, for example, celebrates especially what constitutes "their architectural authority."[6]

Others seem fascinated by their presence, their miraculous existence. Yves Bonnefoy explains to us that Giacometti "was fascinated by the mysterious act by which things are in being before falling back so quickly into nothingness."[7]

Hence the relentlessness of Giacometti and others in despoiling their object of their natural appearances. Disregarding the habitual data of space, Giacometti *geometrizes, deforms, abstracts* his object, magnifying their measurements in order to grasp this mystery.

To contemplate their essences, to be astounded at the presence of things, is to seek the most necessary thing for our spiritual hunger. Essence is the force that organizes matter, raises it up in its architecture, makes it appear in the light like a rose. Existence, at first sight, is common. It is the most hidden element of all. Still, it is the one endowed with the greatest energy. It buttresses itself upon very nothingness. But only the intellect, that "bee of the invisible," can gather it in the depths of things.

It certainly seems that it is the Bible alone that gives us to see existence as a power that snatches each and every thing from nothingness! It is to the Bible that we owe the unveiling of existence. Neither Parmenides, nor Plato, nor Aristotle himself has perceived it for itself. But, as St. Thomas Aquinas notes: "At times, God miraculously instructs certain persons on matters which natural reason could know by its own powers. Just so, God sometimes miraculously produces certain effects that nature nevertheless can realize" (*Summa Theologiae* I–II, q. 109, a. 1).

Let us underscore the word "miraculously" in this "scintillating lesson." With it, this lesson teaches us that God alone produces existence. This is what God has done in "creating" the world.

To perceive existence as a gift is to perceive a "miracle"!

But how can we bring existence to light? How are we to render "sensible" this very first intelligible object? We must come to it by way of nothingness, say the existentialists. It is by nothingness, experienced in and by an affective key of anguish or tedium, of nausea—by a subjective mood, they tell us. But then how will it not appear subjectively, clad in this key? In order to grasp existence, surely we must pass by way of nothing, but it will be the nothing that we think. Our concept of nothingness does not deserve Martin Heidegger's criticism. He does not give us an "abstract nothingness" that would leave us indifferent. On the contrary, only this concept of nothingness gives us to understand the absence of a thing, the absence of the rose. This concept gives us to understand that in order to appear, a thing must traverse the abyss (Greek *a-byssos,* "without bottom," without support).

It is the Bible's great pedagogy to offer us suggestive images in order that we may come to "see" that existence can only have God for its cause.

Indeed, existence is the perfection that must be "drawn" from nothingness. No creature has claims on it. The Bible says it felicitously:

> Even the nations are like a drop from a bucket,
>   and are accounted as dust on the scales;
>   see, he takes up the isles like fine dust. . . .
> All the nations are as nothing before him;
>   they are accounted by him as less than nothing
>   and emptiness. (Isaiah 40:15–17)

And the mother in the second book of the Martyrs of Israel says to the youngest of her sons: "I conjure you, my child, regard the sky and the earth, and see all that is in them, and know that God has made them from *nothing* and that the race of human beings is made in the same fashion" (2 Macc. 7:28).

Perspectives

W E ARE LEFT WITH ONE QUESTION. What relationships does this philosophy maintain with Judeo-Christian revelation? Martin Heidegger, self-styled "shepherd of being," confided to an audience of college teachers: "If I were to write a theology, I should never employ the word 'being.' It was a great error on the part of Western thought to take 'being' for God, an error that has even crept into the Bible."[1]

We answer him: A like assertion separates the speaker altogether from Christian theology. After all, the God of the Exodus, besought by Moses to pronounce his name, responds: "I am who I am" (Exod. 3:14). Of course, the fact remains—and there is no harm in saying it—that, in this cultural context, to give this formula a metaphysical tenor is to engage in a contradiction. Still, a scholarly historian of Semitic and Assyrian religions can say: This name, Yahweh, could make one think of the verb that, in the old Israelite idiom, meant "exist," "be."[2] It is not so incongruous, then, to say, apropos of this definition, that Exodus contains an encounter between a metaphysics of being and the Judeo-Christian revelation.

Let us hear, further, what a theologian observes apropos of this verb:

> In the Old Testament, . . . "to be" (*aya*) expresses the unity of being in becoming, and free and autonomous acting. It belongs to the class of active internal verbs (verbs of state) that become comprehensible to us in the act of being of a person who acts in the freedom of his act. If God states his Name in this Verb, he is expressing the very act in which he presents himself as a free and acting person, setting afoot his designs on the world and on his chosen people.[3]

In light of this reflection, we understand that the same author can conclude: "The revelation of the name [of God] in Exodus [3:14] is not to be dismissed as readily as one thinks."[4]

In the Greek of St. John we hear Jesus using the same verb: "When you have lifted up the Son of Man, then you will realize that I am he" (John 8:27). Clearly, we are dealing with a repetition of the definition in Exodus.

After these data, how could we fail to conclude, with the same theologian: "The divine Name revealed is surely the one that founds the world metaphysically"?[5]

No, one cannot do a Christian theology without the verb "to be."

In his *Summa Theologiae,* St. Thomas Aquinas comments on the formula "He who is," with the following observations (I, q. 13, a. 11).

The name "He who is" is the most proper name for God because it does not denote a particular form of being. God's form and essence are to exist. Second, this name is universal. It does not close God up within the limits of a being. It allows God "to be" in its general sense. This name has the advantage of suggesting that God is the Ocean of Being. The name "He who is" does not determine any mode of being. It denotes not the being that thinks, that speaks, that creates, but the being who "is"—the Being who by nature performs the act of existing, the act of being.

On the basis of this revelation, "He who is," we have new perspectives on the relationships that weave theology and philosophy together.

In the first place, this definition gives us an understanding of the fact that it is precisely in this object that the bodies of wisdom ought to meet. But to understand it, we must attribute all of its force to the manner in which St. Thomas Aquinas speaks to us of the relationship of the intellect to being. "What the intellect conceives as the object best known, and that in which it resolves all of its conceptions, is *being*" (*De Veritate* q. 11, a. 1).

Now, we know that, for St. Thomas, being is constituted by two acts in conjunction, essence and existence. Thus, the very first object of the human intellect is being—these two acts, which constitute all natural things. It is by these natural things that being makes its entry into our intellect, which is bonded to the body. But the intellect understands at the same time that nothing militates against modes of being other than the material mode. And thus "being," the object of the intellect, can span all generic and specific realizations—even cross their frontiers and be applied to a "being" no longer confined within the limits of matter.

Of these two components that constitute being, one is existence. It is the one that brings us the perception of "presence" of the being. The other gives us the "sense," or "meaning," of this being. The "presence" is given to the mind that receives the being as being the other *qua* other, the other *as* other. But each being becomes "present" as the vehicle of a "sense" belonging to it and that it can put to work thanks to existence. But while we see immediately that "this sense," that is, its essence, is an element realized in the thing by virtue of its own powers, existence, by contrast, appears as not being in its powers. And it is in this, most often, that the being of things offers us something like a gift, like a miracle. Jacques Maritain comments:

> It is not a miracle, it is a piece of good fortune, a gift of nature suddenly received, . . . a moment of natural contemplation in which thought is exempted from abstraction. . . . Then the bolt of the intuition of being springs up all of a sudden: this rose exists.[6]

Here we should like to adduce three testimonials, from three very different writers, which will show that these intuitions are not so very rare.

The first, Antoine de Saint-Exupéry, in his *Citadelle* (citadel), says in several places that he has experienced the presence of the One who connects all things together. Like a melodic theme, the expression recurs: "the divine knot that binds things." For Saint-Exupéry, it is the relationships between things that reveal the Presence.

> If you mix up the letters, you erase the poet. And if the garden is no more than a gathering of plants, you erase the gardener. The order, the rapport among things—that is what reveals the gardener.[7]

And God appears as the one who knots things: "It is like an apparition added to things and dominating them, and if it escapes your intelligence, it appears nevertheless as evident to your mind and your heart."[8]

And Saint-Exupéry adds:

> I habitually regard a tree as "true" when it is a certain relation among its parts. Then the forest is a certain relation among the trees. . . . Then God, who is a certain perfect relation among the empires and everything else in the world. God is as true as the tree, although more difficult to read. . . . I know no other truth at all. I know only structures. . . . It has sometimes seemed to me that they bore a resemblance to something.[9]

That is, to a face. "It is then that my geometer-God shows himself."[10]

As for Sartre, either he was unable to see things in this fashion or did not know how to go about it. The garden of Bouville, which he visited often, gave him the impression of a "vile marmalade." But then one day he appeared there as a true "looker."

Then the garden smiled at me. I leaned against the grilled fence and watched, for a long time. The smile of the trees, of the bundling laurel, *meant* something. It was the veritable secret of existence. I recalled that, of a Sunday, not more than three weeks before, I had already seized in things a sort of conspiring air. Was it to me that it was addressed? I felt with annoyance that I had no means of understanding. No means. Still, it was there, waiting. It resembled a look. It was there on the trunk of the chestnut. . . . It was the chestnut, the things, one would have said thoughts that stopped along the route and had forgotten themselves, had forgotten what they had wished to think and who just stayed there shaking, with a funny little meaning that was beyond them. That annoyed me, that funny little meaning: I could not understand it were I to stay a hundred and seventy years leaning on the grill. I had learned about existence all that I could know. I left.[11]

After Saint-Exupéry's reflections, how could we not be struck by the fact that the same context can engender opposite intuitions, depending on the purity of one's intellect!

Another testimonial, that of Aleksandr Solzhenitsyn, will tell us that a single tree can take us back to the first day of the creation of the world. It is in these terms that his novel *The Cancer Ward* ends. Discharged from the hospital, Oleg, the hero of the novel, wishes to go to contemplate an apricot tree that reveals to him the first day of creation:

Then, from the balcony of the house, he noticed a pink sphere. It was the apricot tree. He leaned against the balustrade, and from this dominant position, watched, endlessly watched, the transparent pink marvel. He gave it to himself as a gift in honor of the day of creation. . . . Oleg observed. The rose was the general impression. The apricot tree bore purple buttons similar to little candles. The petals, once they had opened, had a pink exterior and once they had opened, were just plain white, like those of the apple or cherry. Out came this tender rosebush, and Oleg made an effort to absorb it, by his glance. He was awaiting a miracle, and the miracle had taken place.[12]

We shall have noted the expressions of miracle, of marvels, of creation. Once more a tree, but this time by its beauty, leads, right to the creation, and hence to God, the person who regards it in a spirit of wonder. As we shall have noted, it is the presence of God, and the meaning that God gives things, that things are capable of showing.

We should like to contribute the testimonial of painters as well. In a letter to his brother Theo, van Gogh said: "As for me, I find in many modern canvasses a particular charm that the ancients do not have." He thought that the reason for this lay in "the modern artists' be[ing] perhaps greater thinkers."[13] This astonishing reflection on van Gogh's part invites us to do justice to modern painting and sculpture, and to understand them better. Indeed, in Brancusi, Giacometti, and certain cubist painters, there is a kind of need to surpass the représention of things in order the better to grasp the Presence. Yves Bonnefoy speaks in this vein. Brancusi and the cubist painters try to catch the essence of things. They situate that essence beyond natural appearances. There is still more with Giacometti, who seeks the very being of the thing. The deformation, geometrization, abstraction, and elongation of natural forms signal precisely this effort to capture the essential, and capture it in depth. Van Gogh added that one must "feel the things themselves."[14] To capture a ray of the divine gaze upon things, or the traces of God's passage there, defines this attempt of art that, try as it may, cannot take leave of things altogether. It is impossible to separate oneself from them.

To return to metaphysics, we shall say that these two forces that constitute the being of a thing (essence and existence) have been seen by Aristotle. But he has not seen existence as such. He has not seen that existence is an act absolutely different from all other acts, like that of singing, speaking, or thinking. Such acts suppose faculties, existent powers that these acts determine and enrich along the lines of their essence. But with respect to what constitutes the first essence of a thing, its substantial form—what makes this flower a rose or this bird a titmouse—existence presupposes nothingness. These things are created. They come from nothing. Existence is the very first of acts. It is not in the virtue or power of the essence of things. Existence is an irreducible act. It is what Jacques Maritain calls "an irreducible absolute." And he goes on with his characterization: "It is a sort of miracle of nature, which supposes in reality the activity of God as creator, who gives being to all that is."[15]

Existence itself is what St. Thomas has seen and contemplated. But he had the help of biblical revelation, as we have seen. Existence is a concrete attribute, a "perfection," that of itself remains an object of natural reason; but natural reason has not actually found it. It has been miraculously turned toward it by God, who at the same time, and precisely thereby, has engaged in a self-revelation as the per-se-subsistent Being—and that at the "first" and the "second" Passover. It is the exodal and paschal revelation.

Let us recall that God was in no wise obliged to create things—in which existence precisely is not a property of their essence nor a datum of their essence, because they have begun to be and will cease to be—and that therefore no reasoning can deduce the existence of things a priori. All things are the effect of a pure gift of God. And it is precisely in this area in God who transcends all human reason that there is place for a free promise of alliance or covenant with human beings, with a creation that God will have freely decreed. It is in this sense that one must read Jacques Maritain's counsel:

If we would awaken to our existentiality, it is permissible to read
Mr. Heidegger. But we shall do better, in any case, to read the
Bible. The behavior of the Patriarchs, of Moses, of David, of
Job, and of Ezekiel before God will teach us what named exis-
tence is, the existence of the "I."[16]

"**N**amed existence!" Yes, God gave his name, once in
Exodus when he said, "I am who I am," and a second time in
St. John, where Christ reveals himself as the Son in defining
himself: "I am." And at the same time, Christ was teaching us
that the *Being* of the exodus is Father. Being received its
authentic face. Its absolute freedom took on the visage of a
pure gratuity when it created all things from nothing. And to
boot, in Christ, in St. John, God reveals that he is the Father:
"The Gospel of Saint John, in particular, presents Christ's
Passover as the locus of the revelation of the divine Name as
that revelation began at the time of the Exodus."

Père Le Guillou writes: "It is in Christ's Passover that the
sovereign act of being of the divine Name is glorified—when,
in his perfect obedience to the death, Christ reveals that this
name is that of the Father."[17]

Indeed, Christ proclaims it. "When you have lifted up the
Son of Man, then you will realize that I am he, and that I do
nothing on my own, but I speak these things as the Father
instructed me. And the one who sent me is with me" (John
8:28–29).

And we hold to this conclusion:

It is impossible to reject, in the name of theology, this evident
"compromise" of the Passover with Being, and hence the relationship between what it reveals to us of the divine Being and
what metaphysical thought strives to understand on the subject
of being. In the Trinitarian testimonial of Passover, the divine
Name revealed is clearly the one who forms the metaphysical
ground of the world.[18]

There is no place where theology and metaphysics, while retaining their proper objects and insights, more appropriately meet in order to shed light on the relations of God to the world and of the world to God.

We shall not be surprised if, among those who will do us the honor of reading us, some will find a fatal omission in this study. This work is supported by no critique of knowledge. After idealism, then surrounded as we are by Husserlian phenomology, how can one pretend to go to being with this naive confidence? Would it not have been necessary to give the reasons for which we claim the right to speak of the being of things?

We answer that we understand the criticism and accept it. But we nevertheless embrace a primitive realism. The reason for this is things themselves. We have questioned things first, as the reader knows. It is upon their immediate data that we have based our book. We have watched them build themselves—which they do, still, even after the subjectivist crisis! And we have sought to transmit a feeling of the presence of being that is also given immediately with sensations. We have followed Aristotle's lesson. Apropos of Parmenides and Heraclitus, who were the first to cast doubt on the value of our powers of knowing, Aristotle said: "It would have sufficed to regard nature to dissipate their contempt."[19]

We have also been encouraged by Jacques Maritain. In his *The Peasant of the Garonne* he writes: "If the mind seeks to be delivered from the chains that so long have held it captive, what it ought to reject for good and all is the Kantian error."[20]

The intellect assents to the simplicity of the true. It becomes available, and uncharged, and open enough to hear "what all things murmur."[21] And at the same time as we were trusting these masters of realism, we were listening to the poets and contemplating the work of modern painters. We have heard them speak to us, in depth, of "mute things." And in painting and sculpture we were astounded to see them place things in a space more true—in the nontemporal.

Throughout the composition of this book, we have had the support of the reflection of a contemplative on the subject of the modern critique, with special reference to Sartre in *Being and Nothingness.* That contemplative writes, in a letter to us:

> To me, all of these systems seem child's games. I admit it. Mr. Sartre has told us how he believes (or tries to believe) what things are. But the intellect awakens the day it wonders, "What is being?" All of these tableaus, all of these scribblings, these propositions on what can happen or not happen between objects and subjects, etc., it understands as a limpid firmament posing this one question. And it finds its response in the most immediate, the purest part of itself: it perceives that it knows one thing: "By nature, the intellect knows nothing but being and what of itself has a relationship to being." And in the simplicity of this point, on which, as on an invisible fulcrum, it weighs the universe, it can already perceive the divine oneness whose vision is promised to it.

Notes

Introduction

1. Paul Claudel, *La Messe là-bas* (Paris: Gallimard, 1947), 12–13.
2. Paul Claudel, *La Messe là-bas* (La Pléiade, 1957), 498.
3. See nn. 3, 4 of the Tricot edition.
4. Jacques Maritain, *Sept leçons sur l'être* (Paris: Tequi, 1934), 97.
5. Jean-Pierre Torrell, O.P., *Saint Thomas d'Aquin, maître spirituel,* Initiation 2 (Paris: Cerf; Fribourg: Editions Universitaires, 1996), 574.
6. Ibid., 305.
7. Ibid., 310.
8. Ibid., 39.
9. Charles Journet, *Connaissance et Inconnaissance de Dieu* (Editions St.-Augustin, 1996), 21–22.
10. Jacques Maritain, *Art et Scholastique* (Paris: L. Rouart, 1927), 145.
11. Theophile, *Nova et Vetera* (1944): 331–32.

Part 1

1. Georges du Plain, *C.-F. Ramuz* (Editions 24 Heures), 398.
2. Jacques Maritain, *Approches sans entraves* (Paris: Fayard, 1973), 98.
3. Du Plain, *Ramuz,* 261.

4. C.-F. Ramuz, *Présence de la mort,* 59.

5. Rainer Maria Rilke, *Poèmes français* (Paris: Emile Paul, 1944), 131.

6. Ibid., 126.

7. Saint-John Perse, *Oiseaux* (Paris: Gallimard, 1963).

8. Malebranche, *Recherche de la vérité,* book 6, part 2, chap. 3.

9. Cited by S. Fumet, *Le néant contesté* (Paris: Fayard, 1972), 123.

10. Jacques Maritain, *Sept leçons sur l'être* (Paris: Tequi, 1934), 148; Aristotle, *Metaphysics* 11.1072a.28.

11. Jacques Maritain, *Court traité de l'existence et de l'existant* (Paris: Hartmann, 1947), 42.

12. Paul Claudel, *Deuxième Ode* (La Pléiade, 1962), 239.

13. Paul Claudel, *La cantate à trois voix* (La Pléiade, 1962), 334.

14. Cited in Jean-Luc Barré, *Jacques et Raïssa Maritain: Les Mendiants du Ciel* (Paris: Stock, 1995), 103.

15. Claudel, *Deuxième Ode,* 238–39.

16. Cardinal Charles Journet, *Entretiens sur le Mystère chrétien,* 1:134.

17. Translation of Philippe Jaccottet (Rencontre, 1951), 117–18.

18. Rilke, *Poèmes français,* 145.

19. G. K. Chesterton, *Orthodoxie* (Paris: Gallimard, 1984), 95.

20. Journet, *Entretiens,* 1:148.

21. C.-F. Ramuz, *Remarques: L'Age d'Homme* (1987), 72.

22. Claudel, *La Messe là-bas* (La Pléiade), 522.

Part 2

1. Paul Claudel, *Deuxième Ode* (La Pléiade, 1962), 238.

2. In this part of our book, we refer to our *The Dearest Freshness Deep Down Things: An Introduction to the Philosophy of Being* (New York: Crossroad, 1999), where the principal concepts employed here have been expounded more completely.

3. Rainer Maria Rilke, *Oeuvres,* vol. 2, *Poésie* (1972), 508, strophe 20.

4. Jacques Maritain, *Approches sans entraves* (Paris: Fayard, 1973), 270.

5. Ionesco, *La Quête intermittente* (Paris: Gallimard, 1987), 106.

6. *Cahiers de Jacques Maritain*, no. 20 (1955): 34 (emphasis mine).

7. Trans. Yves Battisini, *Trois contemporains* (Paris: Gallimard, 1955), 93.

8. See *Fragments,* 15, *Les Présocratiques.*

Part 3

1. Charles Journet, *Connaissance et Inconnaissance de Dieu* (Editions St.-Augustin, 1996), 77.

2. Ibid., 17.

3. For this entire chapter, see Jacques Maritain, *Sept leçons sur l'être* (Paris: Tequi, 1934), 71–75.

4. Jacques Maritain, *La philosophie de la nature* (Paris: Tequi, 1935), 29.

5. Charles Baudelaire, *Correspondance* (La Pléiade), 11.

6. Ibid., 18.

7. Anne Perrier, *Les noms de l'arbre* (Lausanne: Empreintes, 1989).

8. St. John of the Cross, *Poèmes mystiques* (Neuchâtel: Cahiers du Rhône), 15–17.

9. St. John of the Cross, *Le Cantique spirituel,* "A" (Paris: Cerf, 1981), 84.

10. Jacques Maritain, *L'intuition créatrice dans l'art et la poésie* (Paris: Desclée de Brouwer, 1966), 28.

11. Rudiger Safranski, *Heidegger et son temps* (Grasset), 172.

12. Jean Bottero, *Naissance de Dieu* (Paris: N.R.F. and Gallimard), 41.

13. Ibid., 48.

14. Jean-Paul Sartre, *L'Être et le néant* (Paris: N.R.F. and Gallimard), 31.

15. Charles Journet, "La Présence de Dieu dans le monde" (photocopy), 15.

Part 4

1. *Angelus Silesius,* book 5, trans. into French by Dom J.-B. Porrion.

2. Ibid.

3. Jacques Maritain, *Art et Scolastique: Les Frontières de la poésie* (Paris: L. Rouart, 1927), 145.

4. Paul Claudel, *Mémoires improvisés* (Paris: Gallimard and N.R.F., 1954), 192.

5. Père Sertillanges, O.P., *Dieu,* 2:403. French translation.

6. Charles Baudelaire, *Le Confiteor de l'artiste* (La Pléiade).

7. Jean-Paul Sartre, *L'existentialisme est un humanisme* (Nagel, 1946), 9–25.

8. Sertillanges, *Dieu,* 2:352 n. 111. French translation.

9. Dialogue with Jean Beauffret.

10. Jean-Paul Sartre, *L'Être et le néant* (Paris: N.R.F. and Gallimard), 31.

11. Jacques Maritain, *Philosophie morale* (Paris: Gallimard and N.R.F., 1960).

12. *Paul Claudel interroge l'Apocalypse* (Paris: N.R.F.)

13. Cardinal Charles Journet, *Entretiens sur le Mystère chrétien,* vol. 1.

14. Ibid.

General Conclusion

1. Saint-John Perse, *Poésie* (Paris: Gallimard, 1961), 2.

2. Ibid., 2–3.

3. Anne Perrier, "A la Rose" *Nova et Vetera* (1970): 223–27.

4. Jacques Maritain, *Les degrés du savoir* (Paris: Desclée de Brouwer), 5.

5. Paul Claudel, *Cantate à trois voix* (Paris: N.R.F., 1931), 23.

6. Jacques Maritain, *L'intuition créatrice dans l'art et la poésie* (Paris: Desclée, 1966), 28.

7. Yves Bonnefoy, *Alberto Giacometti* (Flammarion, 1991).

Perspectives

1. Georges Brazzola, *Nova et Vetera* (1982): 67.

2. Jean Bottero, *Naissance de Dieu* (Paris: N.R.F. and Gallimard), 41.

3. M.-J. Le Gillou, O.P., *Le Mystère du Père* (Paris: Fayard), 227.

4. Ibid., 22.

5. Ibid., 228.

6. Jacques Maritain, *Approches sans entraves* (Paris: Fayard, 1973), 270.

7. Antoine de Saint-Exupéry, *Citadelle* (La Pléiade, 1959), 714.

8. Ibid., 746.

9. Ibid., 783.

10. Ibid., 784.

11. Jean-Paul Sartre, *La nausée* (Paris: Gallimard, 1938), 190.

12. Aleksandr Solzhenitsyn, *The Cancer Ward* (Julliard, 1968), 644–45.

13. *Lettres de Vincent van Gogh* (Grasset, 1937).

14. Ibid., 66.

15. Maritain, *Approches sans entraves*, 282.

16. *Cahiers Jacques Maritain* (Kollsheim), 6:7.

17. Le Guillou, *Mystére du Pére*, 228.

18. Ibid.

19. Aristotle, *Physics*, trans. Henri Carteron (Les Belles lettres), p. 48 (191b.33–34).

20. Jacques Maritain, *Le Paysan de la Garonne* (Paris: Desclée de Brouwer), 163.

21. Ibid., 164.

OF RELATED INTEREST

The Rule of Benedict: A Spirituality for the 21st Century

ISBN: 9780824525941 / (Paperback)

Today's major spiritual inquiries such as stewardship, relationships, authority, community, balance, work, simplicity, prayer and psychological development are all addressed in this five-hundred-year-old classic known as The Rule of Benedict. With extraordinary vision and common sense this rule written by Benedict of Nursia, the founder of Western monasticism, guides us into a new way of seeing and living that can transform our modern world just like it did 500 years ago.

For over 30 years, Joan Chittister, O.S.B. has been a passionate and energetic speaker, counselor, and clear voice, for the global community. A Benedictine Sister of Erie, PA, Sister Joan is an international lecturer and award-winning author of over 40 books, and the founder and executive director of Benetvision.

Support your local bookstore or order directly from the publisher at
www.CrossroadPublishing.com

To request a catalog or inquire about quantity orders, please e-mail
sales@CrossroadPublishing.com

Crossroad